President's Commission on Organized Crime

Interim Report to the President
and the
Attorney General

THE CASH CONNECTION:
Organized Crime,
Financial Institutions,
and Money Laundering

Books for Business
New York- Hong Kong

The Cash Connection: Organized Crime, Financial
Institutions, and Money Laundering

by
President's Commission on Organized Crime

ISBN: 0-89499-105-1

Reprinted from the 1985 edition

Books for Business
New York - Hong Kong
http://www.BusinessBooksInternational.com

PRESIDENT'S COMMISSION ON ORGANIZED CRIME

Suite 700
1425 K Street, NW
Washington, D.C. 20005
202-786-3500

Suite 2-122
26 Federal Plaza
New York, N.Y. 10278
212-264-3400

Chairman:
Honorable Irving R. Kaufman

Executive Director and
Chief Counsel
James D. Harmon, Jr.

Commissioners:
Jesse A. Brewer, Jr.
Carol Corrigan
Justin J. Dintino
William J. Guste, Jr.
Judith R. Hope
Philip R. Manuel
Thomas F. McBride
Eugene H. Methvin
Edwin L. Miller, Jr.
Manuel J. Reyes
Honorable Peter W. Rodino, Jr.
Charles H. Rogovin
Barbara A. Rowan
Frances A. Sclafani
Samuel K. Skinner
Honorable Potter Stewart
Honorable Strom Thurmond
Phyllis T. Wunsche

Honorable Ronald Reagan
President of the United States
The White House
Washington, D.C. 20500

Dear Mr. President:

Pursuant to Executive Order 12435 and Public Law 98-368, I present the first interim report of the President's Commission on Organized Crime. Since I accepted your appointment as Chairman of this Commission, the members of the Commission and I have become increasingly dismayed by the virtual impunity with which organized criminal enterprises and their members and affiliates "launder" the proceeds of their illegal activities through financial institutions in this country and abroad. This abuse of our financial system by career criminals has become a nationwide affliction, and thoroughly deserves the condemnation it has received from law enforcement officials and members of the business community.

This interim report, which examines the problems of money laundering in the United States by organized crime, is the culmination of a concerted effort by the members and staff of the Commission. The report sets forth a number of substantial administrative and legislative recommendations, as well as suggestions for voluntary action by the private sector.

As our study reveals, money laundering is the lifeblood of organized crime. The Commission believes that its recommendations, when implemented, will arm the financial community and law enforcement authorities with the weapons needed to strike at the very heart of the narcotics trade and other activities engaged in by organized criminal groups. The driving force of organized crime is the incentive to earn vast sums of money; without the ability to freely utilize its ill-gotten gains, the underworld will have been dealt a crippling blow.

Sincerely,

Irving R. Kaufman
Chairman

TABLE OF CONTENTS

EXECUTIVE SUMMARY

This first report of the Commission examines the problem of money laundering, the means by which one conceals the existence, illegal source, or illegal application of income, and then disguises that income to make it appear legitimate. While concealment of enormous amounts of illegally generated income would seem to pose a formidable challenge to organized criminal groups, professional money launderers have been known to launder hundreds of millions of dollars of these proceeds with virtual impunity.

Section One of the report details the problems of money laundering and law enforcement authorities' response to it. The scope of money laundering is evidenced by the broad array of participants—ranging from La Cosa Nostra members to casinos, motorcycle gangs, and Fortune 500 companies—seeking to launder money. Although it is difficult to determine exactly how much money is laundered annually, tracing the cash flow between the United States and foreign countries provides an indication of the level of laundering activity.

The principal tool now utilized to detect, measure, and punish money laundering is the Bank Secrecy Act. The Act requires that a Currency Transaction Report (CTR) must be filed by financial institutions whenever a currency transaction is more than $10,000. In addition, a Currency or Monetary Instrument Report (CMIR) must be filed whenever currency or monetary instruments of more than $5,000 are taken into or out of the United States. Finally, a Foreign Bank Account Report (FBAR) is required whenever a person has an account in a foreign bank of more than $5,000. Although the Bank Secrecy Act has provided an effective way to deter the activities of money laundering, its effectiveness has been limited because of problems in the means by which the Act is administered and because of actions by certain financial institutions.

Once a customer of a financial institution is suspected of engaging in money laundering, there is a considerable delay before this information is confirmed. This is due to the reticence of financial institutions to inform law enforcement authorities of suspicious transactions, the time required to process CTRs and CMIRs, and the restrictions placed on the Treasury Department in transferring CTR and CMIR data to other Federal agencies. Furthermore, the Treasury Department alone bears the responsibility of monitoring and investigating money laundering. Other agencies that could provide additional investigative experience and resources have been unable to share some of that responsibility because they lack jurisdiction.

Under the Bank Secrecy Act, Federal agencies lack important investigative techniques and resources which could be used effectively against money launderers. These include the use of court-authorized electronic surveillance for violations of the Act. In addition, there is an insufficient number of FBI, DEA, and IRS agents available to investigate money laundering-related violations. Finally, the effectiveness of the Bank Secrecy Act is limited because the civil and criminal penalties imposed by the Act are far too lenient to punish and deter money laundering. Unless a pattern of violations can be demonstrated, the Treasury Department can impose a civil penalty of no more than $1,000 per violation, and Federal courts can sentence defendants to no more than one year in prison and $1,000 per violation. This does not pose a significant threat to the individual whose laundering schemes have limitless financial potential.

Section Two of the report sets forth a number of case studies that demonstrate the diversity and magnitude of money laundering schemes. For example:

- In the Pizza Connection case, La Cosa Nostra members distributed heroin imported from Southeast Asia's Golden Triangle through pizza parlors in the United States, and then transferred the cash generated through New York to Switzerland and finally to Italy, where it was used to buy more heroin. Authorities estimate that at least $25 million was laundered between October 1980 and September 1982.
- In the Great American Bank case, officers and employees of the bank received a fee for processing large amounts of cash without filing the required CTRs. More than $94 million was laundered by the bank from December 1982 through April 1984 for the depositors, three narcotics organizations.
- People's Liberty Bank of Covington, Kentucky was involved in the laundering scheme of a Colombian citizen, Luis Pinto, who was involved in a cocaine ring. Pinto made large cash deposits, often close to $300,000 at a time, and made withdrawals in the form of bank drafts or cashier's checks, usually in amounts that did not require the filing of CTRs. Pinto frequently made withdrawals of $10,000 from several different branches in a single day to circumvent reporting requirements. Despite the suspect nature of Pinto's transactions, the bank never notified local or Federal law enforcement agencies.

These and other case studies highlighted in the report make clear that while money laundering schemes may be difficult for law enforcement agencies to detect, those involving insider collusion are the most difficult. Furthermore, the deliberate indifference to suspect transactions demonstrated by some bank employees furthers money laundering. Also, Federal law enforcement authorities may not have access to needed information about a customer from a financial institution in an investigation of a laundering scheme because the Right to Financial Privacy Act does not authorize such disclosure. Finally, in some cases financial institutions have informed customers that they are the subject of a criminal investigation, thus hindering the conduct of these investigations.

Section Three of the report sets forth the Commission's administrative and legislative recommendations, as well as recommendations for voluntary action by financial institutions, to deal more effectively with money laundering. These proposed voluntary guidelines for the banking community are designed to help ensure that financial institutions' internal policies do not make them easy prey for money launderers. Either a branch manager or assistant manager should be made ultimately responsible for completion of the CTR and should be required to countersign the CTR. Tellers, officers and other employees should be trained more extensively both in the requirements of the Bank Secrecy Act and in the features common to money laundering. Financial institutions should implement an internal clearinghouse for all CTRs and CMIRs generated in branch commercial activities so that management can review compliance at an early stage.

In addition, customers who wish to be exempted from the Bank Secrecy Act's reporting requirements should be subjected to background investigations as stringent as those conducted on loan applicants. The decision to grant an exemption should be approved by at least two bank officers. Furthermore, special attention should be paid to activities which have been used in laundering schemes but which often evade review, such as the purchase or cashing of cashier's checks and deposits or exchange of large amounts of currency by an individual in a fiduciary relationship with the account holder.

The Commission's administrative recommendations include the use of CTR, CMIR, and FBAR data by the Treasury Department to determine which countries are most likely to be used in money laundering schemes, so that the Justice Department can focus its investigations on these areas; the granting of additional manpower and resources to the IRS, the FBI, and the DEA to investigate money laundering more effectively; the implementation of a procedure by the Secretary of the Treasury and financial institutions to expedite the process by which the institutions inform law enforcement authorities of violations of the

Act; the adoption of a procedure by the Treasury Department to discourage financial institutions from abusing the authority to grant customers exemptions from the requirements of the Act; and the inclusion of casinos in the Treasury Department regulations' definition of financial institutions under the Act.

The Commission's legislative recommendations include the passage of amendments to the Right to Financial Privacy Act that would permit a financial institution to disclose certain information to a law enforcement agency, to permit the agency to determine whether a formal investigation is warranted, and that ensure that financial institutions would not be subject to private damage actions for such disclosures or for failure to notify customers of such disclosures; amendments to the Bank Secrecy Act that would permit the Secretary of the Treasury to offer rewards for information regarding violations leading to penalties under the Act, and to transfer information from CTRs, CMIRs, or FBARs to other agencies as necessary for an investigation; amendments to the Bank Secrecy Act that would increase civil and criminal penalties for violations of the Act; and an amendment to Title III of the Omnibus Crime Control and Safe Streets Act of 1968, to include the criminal provisions of the Bank Secrecy Act as a predicate for the issuance of judicial orders authorizing interception of telephone calls, telexes, and other forms of wire or oral communications.

While these recommendations, if effected, could significantly enhance the ability of law enforcement authorities to hinder money laundering activity, none of them addresses the problem of money laundering directly. The money launderer who complies with the recordkeeping and reporting requirements of the Bank Secrecy Act, as has often been done, cannot be prosecuted unless it has been proven that he has violated another Federal statute. This report therefore proposes draft legislation, denominated the Financial Institutions Protection Act, that includes provisions to make the use of financial institutions by money launderers a criminal offense. Such legislation would give Federal law enforcement agents the authority to investigate money launderers and their couriers from the time that they enter financial institutions.

The Commission invites the response of the banking community to these recommendations and proposed legislation. Constructive dialogue between law enforcement and financial institutions is essential to the development of new procedures and legislation which will deny money launderers access to financial institutions for their illegally generated profits.

THE PRESIDENT'S COMMISSION ON ORGANIZED CRIME

The President's Commission on Organized Crime was established by Executive Order 12435 on July 28, 1983. The Executive Order directs the Commission to:

- Make a full and complete national and region-by-region analysis of organized crime;
- Define the nature of traditional organized crime as well as emerging organized crime groups, the sources and amounts of organized crime's income, and the uses to which organized crime puts its income;
- Develop in-depth information on the participants in organized crime networks;
- Evaluate Federal laws pertinent to the effort to combat organized crime;
- Advise the President and the Attorney General with respect to its findings and actions which can be undertaken to improve law enforcement efforts directed against organized crime;
- Make recommendations concerning appropriate administrative and legislative improvements and improvements in the administration of justice; and
- Report to the President from time to time as requested, and to submit its final report by March 1, 1986.

The Commission is authorized to issue subpoenas for the testimony of witnesses and the production of information, to issue orders compelling testimony over a claim of the privilege against self-incrimination, and to seek the assistance of the Department of Justice in applying for writs of habeas corpus ad testificandum or judicial orders requiring testimony or the production of information before the Commission. In addition, the Commission may obtain, use, and disclose electronic surveillance data obtained by law enforcement agencies under Title III of the Omnibus Crime Control and Safe Streets Act of 1968, and other information from Federal departments and agencies under the Bank Secrecy Act and the Privacy Act of 1974, as well as from financial institutions under the Right to Financial Privacy Act.

The Commission is composed of nineteen members appointed by the President, including its Chairman, Judge Irving R. Kaufman of the United States Court of Appeals for the Second Circuit. The members of the Commission—who include retired United States Supreme Court Justice Potter Stewart, Senator Strom Thurmond, and Representative Peter W. Rodino, Jr.—come from diverse backgrounds and professions, including several with practical experience in criminal justice and combating organized crime.

INTRODUCTION

The existence of modern, sophisticated, often international services of financial institutions has contributed to the frightening financial successes of organized crime in recent years, particularly in the narcotics trade. Without the means to launder money, thereby making cash generated by a criminal enterprise appear to come from a legitimate source, organized crime could not flourish as it now does. The need to launder money has led organized crime to avail itself of the full range of banking services normally associated with legitimate, multinational businesses. Indeed, a new lexicon—including phrases like wire transfer, bank-to-bank transfer, CTR, CMIR, shell corporation, margin account, and letter of credit—has moved from Wall Street to the back street.

To be sure, many of the banking transactions which facilitate illegal activities appear legitimate, and in these instances the financial institution is an unwitting participant. At other times a suspicious bank employee may be reluctant to voice his concern in the face of bank policy concerning the customer's privacy and a confusing web of state and Federal regulations. In spite of these obstacles, financial institutions have often rendered invaluable assistance to law enforcement authorities. Unfortunately, there are also far too many instances in which officers and employees have actively participated in violations of the law.[1]

The assistance given organized crime through some financial institutions takes many forms, from the corrupt bank president who takes payments from narcotics dealers in return for providing money laundering services, to the head cashier who turns a blind eye as cardboard boxes stuffed with cash are brought into the bank for deposit. Examples of corruption in the banking industry include:

- Officials of the Great American Bank of Florida, who, in return for a percentage of the money deposited, laundered more than $94 million in cash that narcotics dealers brought to the bank in cardboard boxes;
- The president of the Pan American International Bank in Las Vegas who laundered more than $400,000 for an undercover Internal Revenue Service (IRS) agent posing as a corrupt Mexican official and then tutored the agent on how to avoid detection by Federal bank examiners;
- An officer of a Hong Kong bank, who, together with the manager for the bank's San Francisco branch, devised a money laundering

3

scheme for two undercover IRS agents posing as narcotics dealers, that included written instructions on how to frustrate the investigative audit trail. Later the bank accepted an unreported deposit of $442,500 in violation of Federal law.

Although this report will recommend substantial legislative and administrative improvements in the laws applicable to money laundering, ultimately the financial community itself can accomplish the most. If financial institutions deny sanctuary to drug and rackets money, those criminal enterprises will be less profitable and more frequently detected. If, on the other hand, banking services continue to be available to professional criminals whose illegal activities surface only at this vital point, organized crime will continue to take full advantage of those services in concealing its profits.

Denying organized crime access to the financial institutions of this country is a crucial component in a comprehensive attack on drugs. Another vital component is the control and eradication of drugs at their source. The success of the financial component of this attack depends upon a commitment to cooperate by our financial institutions, just as the control of drugs at their source depends upon the competence, capability, and will of foreign governments.

In calling upon our own private sector to turn away the mob's money, we draw upon the strength of our system of free enterprise because there is little reason to expect foreign governments to act if we cannot also secure the assistance of our own financial community.

Although a comprehensive review of our overseas initiatives in this area is beyond the scope of this report, a strike at domestic cash laundering operations should further foreign policy initiatives now underway with source countries, by providing a clear sign that the United States is committed to the idea that our financial institutions shall not profit from organized criminal activity.

Because money laundering plays a vital role in furthering the activities of organized crime, the President's Commission on Organized Crime (the Commission) began an examination of various aspects of the problem of money laundering. Since July 1984, the Commission has made extensive use of the investigative powers that were conferred on it by its enabling legislation, Public Law 98-368, to gather a substantial body of information concerning the scope of, and participants in, money laundering schemes:

- Documents provided by financial institutions that have been used as conduits for money laundering;
- Interviews, conducted by Commission staff, with officials and employees of such financial institutions;

4

- Examination of classified information concerning the international dimensions of money laundering;
- Sworn depositions, conducted by Commission attorneys, of officials and employees of financial institutions, as well as prisoners in Federal custody, who have been involved in money laundering schemes;
- Discussions and interviews, conducted by Commission staff, with officials and employees of various Federal law enforcement and bank supervisory agencies; and
- Testimony of Federal law enforcement officials and agents, members of organized crime groups, and others in the Commission's first two public hearings and in recent Congressional hearings.

In gathering and reviewing this information, the Commission has been mindful of the contributions that the executive and legislative branches have made in recent years to public understanding of the problem. In addition to the numerous successful investigations and prosecutions by the Department of the Treasury and the Department of Justice to enforce the Bank Secrecy Act, several Congressional committees have devoted commendable attention and energy to investigations of specific aspects of money laundering: the Senate Permanent Subcommittee on Investigations, with respect to the criminal use of offshore banks;[2] the House Judiciary Committee's Subcommittee on Crime, with respect to the use of casinos for money laundering; and the House Banking Committee's Subcommittee on General Oversight and Renegotiation, with respect to administration of the Bank Secrecy Act.

As part of the initial phase of the Commission's work in this area, this first report concentrates on the abuse of domestic financial institutions as conduits for the movement of cash or its equivalent generated through illegal narcotics trafficking. Among the principal topics explored in this report are:

- A review of the Bank Secrecy Act, including a brief critical examination of the investigative tools and other resources devoted to financial institutions' compliance, the effectiveness of bank examinations, and the sufficiency of civil and criminal penalties under the Act.
- The basic steps financial institutions should be expected to take to provide important information to law enforcement authorities and to avoid the compromise of ongoing investigations.
- A proposed statute, the Financial Institutions Protection Act, that, for the first time, would make money laundering a crime.

5

This report does not purport to be a definitive treatment of all issues associated with the problem of money laundering. Certain elements of international money laundering, such as the use of foreign banks and the legal impediments created by foreign secrecy and blocking statutes, have been expressly reserved for future consideration, as the Commission continues its program of public hearings and investigation and research by its staff in this area. Nor does it purport to be a comprehensive assessment of the effectiveness of law enforcement agencies in pursuing the problem. It does, however, constitute an invitation to the financial community and the Federal Government to continue and expand the dialogue that they have begun to deal with the problem. By issuing this report, the Commission seeks to develop a closer and continuing collaboration with the Congress, the Treasury Department, and financial institutions in devising a sound and effective program of legislative, administrative, and voluntary actions to combat money laundering.

MONEY LAUNDERING: THE PROBLEM AND THE RESPONSE

WHAT IS MONEY LAUNDERING?

> *Laundering money is to switch the black money, or dirty money . . . [to] clean money . . . .*
>
> Michele Sindona[3]

"Money laundering" is the process by which one conceals the existence, illegal source, or illegal application of income, and then disguises that income to make it appear legitimate.[4] Narcotics traffickers, for example, often seek to change large amounts of cash received from "street-level" sales into an ostensibly legitimate form, such as business profits or loans, before using those funds for personal benefit or reinvesting them in new narcotics purchases and distribution. In addition, corporations otherwise engaged in legitimate commerce may develop surreptitious channels for the use of corporate funds in the payment of commercial bribes or unlawful political contributions.

Law enforcement agencies recognize that narcotics traffickers, who must conceal billions of dollars in cash from detection by the government, create by far the greatest demand for money laundering schemes. It must be noted, however, that numerous other types of activities typical of organized crime, such as loansharking and gambling, also create an appreciable demand for such schemes. Moreover, violations of tax laws are an inevitable byproduct of laundering schemes that conceal the existence or illegal source of income. No matter what type of crime produces the income to be laundered, income tax evasion, with the resulting loss of public revenue, may persist long after the commission of other crimes has ended. In any event, money laundering has become increasingly valuable to organized crime because it enhances and expands the already substantial profitability of the illegal activities in which organized criminal groups engage.

Because a broad spectrum of techniques—many of them completely legal—can be used to launder funds, the suitability of a laundering technique for a particular criminal will depend in part upon the criminal's

7

ultimate objective. At one end of the spectrum, a narcotics trafficker who wishes merely to increase the immediate portability of his cash receipts can simply exchange smaller-denomination bills (*e.g.*, one-, five-, and ten-dollar bills) for larger-denomination bills. At the other end of the spectrum, a high-level member of a large organization that derives vast sums of money from continuing illegal activities will need more sophisticated techniques to conceal those funds for longer periods of time from detection by law enforcement agencies. Such techniques are likely to include multiple international transfers of funds, by various types of financial institutions, to or from foreign countries whose laws, customs, or practices operate (by design or fortuity) to place potentially in-criminating financial and business records beyond the reach of U.S. law enforcement authorities. Such techniques may also include the use of courier services or electronic fund transfers, the processing of funds through layers of fictitious entities, and the creation of false documen-tation to improve the appearance of legitimacy.

Ultimately, the degree of sophistication and complexity in a laundering scheme is virtually infinite, and is limited only by the creative imagina-tion and expertise of the criminal entrepreneurs who devise such schemes. Traditional organized crime, of course, has engaged in some forms of laundering for years, directing its assets through a variety of controlled, legitimate businesses. In recent years, however, an increasing number of persons such as Michele Sindona have mastered the details of modern technology, international finance, and foreign secrecy laws to create a select fraternity of money laundering professionals. As a result, organized crime today uses banks and other financial institutions as routinely, if not as frequently, as legitimate businesses.

THE SCOPE OF THE PROBLEM

Sindona has stated to the Commission that one can launder "a hun-dred thousand dollars (or) a hundred million dollars" in even a single transaction. This statement suggests that the scope of the problem is enormous. In spite of the elaborate recordkeeping systems required by law, no one has yet calculated precisely how much money is laundered. All of the methods available to the Federal Government for measuring the scale and scope of concealing illegal, as well as legal, profits are indirect.

The principal means by which the government can measure, detect, and punish money laundering is the Bank Secrecy Act.[5] Under the Act, financial institutions have the responsibility to report domestic transac-tions of currency or its equivalent in amounts of more than $10,000.[6]

Regulations under the Act, issued by the Secretary of the Treasury, provide law enforcement agencies with four basic tools to investigate money laundering:

- A paper trail of bank records that must be maintained for up to five years.
- A Currency Transaction Report (CTR) that must be filed by banks and other financial institutions whenever a currency transaction is more than $10,000. CTRs are filed with the IRS. Notably omitted from the reporting requirements are wire transfers, bank checks, bank drafts or other written orders of transfer.
- A Currency or Monetary Instruments Report (CMIR) whenever currency or monetary instruments of more than $5,000 are taken into or out of the U.S. CMIRs are filed with the Customs Service. Cashier's checks and bearer bonds made out to cash—rather than to an individual—are not covered by the reporting requirements.
- A Foreign Bank Account Report (FBAR) required whenever a person has an account in a foreign bank of more than $5,000 in value.

Criminal penalties for violations, such as the failure to file a properly completed CTR, are generally misdemeanors but can be elevated to a felony when the violation is part of a pattern of illegal activity involving transactions exceeding $100,000 in any twelve-month period.[7] Civil monetary penalties can be assessed at a maximum of $1,000 per violation.[8]

For most of the first decade after passage of the Act, the Federal Government did not vigorously enforce its provisions.[9] Today, by contrast, the amount of information available from CTRs and CMIRs is so great that it poses a challenge to the effective use of that information. Annual filings of CTRs and CMIRs, as recorded by the Department of the Treasury, reflect a growth of more than 400% in the last 5 years:[10]

CTRs			CMIRs		
Year	Number	Dollar Amount (in Billions)	Year	Number	Dollar Amount (in Billions)
1979	121,000	*	1979	76,909	*
1980	229,000	12.9	1980	114,268	15.3
1981	348,000	17.8	1981	144,704	24.7
1982	425,000	18.6	1982	158,122	30.7
1983	535,000	20.6	1983	185,498	22.9

*Not currently available

9

These filings constitute a vast and constantly growing haystack of information, in which criminal investigators are expected to find the needles that represent criminal proceeds or unreported income being laundered. Because law enforcement agencies need to know where to begin to look for laundered money, information pointing to a particular portion of the haystack (*i.e.,* a particular institution) is invaluable.

The magnitude of the money laundering problem is also evidenced by the variety of schemes and the diversity of participants uncovered since the inception of the Bank Secrecy Act in 1970.

THE ANTHONY SCOTTO CASE

Anthony Scotto, vice-president and general organizer of the International Longshoreman's Association and a member of the Gambino family of La Cosa Nostra, was convicted in 1979 of racketeering, tax evasion, and accepting illegal pay-offs. Scotto received $210,000 over three years from one company in return for his help in reducing fraudulent and exaggerated workmen's compensation claims filed by members of Scotto's local union.

The scheme involved a plan to keep the payments off the company's books by wiring the money from a Philadelphia bank to a bank in Geneva, Switzerland and then back to an account at Brown Brothers Harriman and Co., a private New York bank. Cash drawn from the account was returned to the company via a Chase Manhattan Bank safe deposit box.

THE CARLOS MARCELLO CASE

Joseph Hauser, a former insurance executive, and later a government witness, was convicted in 1979 on Federal charges arising out of a scheme to swindle substantial sums from the International Brotherhood of Teamsters' health, welfare, and pension plans. Hauser was charged with converting $3.5 million in illegal proceeds, about $1.8 million of which was secreted in a Swiss bank account. With Hauser cooperating in an undercover operation, the FBI was able to convict Carlos Marcello, the head of the New Orleans La Cosa Nostra family, for his role in union racketeering.

THE CASINO CASE[11]

In 1983, a Baltimore drug trafficker was convicted of Federal narcotics violations after using an Atlantic City casino to launder his drug profits. The trafficker's network, which consisted of at least sixty to eighty people, included a number of juveniles who worked as "runners," delivering heroin to customers on Mopeds that the trafficker had bought for that purpose.

According to Congressional testimony by W. Hunt Dumont, the United States Attorney for the District of New Jersey, the trafficker and his associates took $118,000 in drug profits to the casino, opened an account, and stayed several days but did not gamble. They left the casino with checks, made payable to third parties, which they deposited in a securities firm. The money was later withdrawn and used to refurbish a number of legitimate businesses owned by the trafficker and his associates.

On still other occasions, the trafficker deposited cash in the casino in small denominations, gambled, and left with most of the cash in $100 bills. At the time that search warrants were executed in the case, $300,000 in $100 bills were found with the casino's wrappers still on the money. Law enforcement authorities have estimated that the trafficker and his group laundered approximately $500,000 in heroin proceeds through the casino in question.[12]

HELL'S ANGELS

Sergei Walton, former head of the Oakland, California chapter of the Hell's Angels, in an interview with the Commission, described the Angels' "buy out, burn out, bomb out" program to launder the profits of its illegal methamphetamine traffic. Walton explained that the gang's profits were laundered by the purchase, through "front men," of failing businesses, thus legitimizing cash from drug sales. Those businesses which resisted the Angels' "buy out" overture were then subjected to the other two-thirds of the outlaw gang's acquisition program.

Walton also described ways in which the Hells' Angels utilize real estate purchases as a means to legitimize and invest these same drug proceeds. Although the Hell's Angels, according to Walton, did not routinely attempt to corrupt bank officials, their business operations involved the flow of illegal monies through financial institutions.

FORTUNE 500 CORPORATIONS

Although the Commission focused on organized crime during its investigation, it became clear that money laundering is not limited to traditional organized crime. Money laundering techniques can be used by large legitimate businesses as well.

Gulf Oil Corporation, Lockheed Aircraft Corporation, and McDonnell Douglas Corporation were each involved in schemes to make illegal payments to foreign government officials in order to win lucrative overseas contracts.

Gulf Oil's payments in excess of $4 million to Korean and Bolivian politicians were capitalized through the yearly disbursement of $500,000 to a corporate subsidiary in the Bahamas. These disbursements, characterized as operating expenses, were funneled back to the United States to be used as bribes by a corporate accountant who carried packages of $25,000 in cash between the Bahamas and the United States.

Lockheed Aircraft's illegal payments totaling $25.5 million between 1969 and 1975 were disguised through false accounting entries and the utilization of cash and "bearer" drafts payable directly to the foreign officials. Deak-Perera Company in Los Angeles facilitated the Japanese briberies by wiring $8.3 million to its Hong Kong office, where the U.S. dollars were changed to Japanese yen and presented to Deak personnel for delivery in Japan.

McDonnell Douglas recouped its illegal payments to high-level Pakistani officials by inflating the cost of each DC10 aircraft sold to Pakistani Airlines. Payoffs to top-level executives of Korean Airlines, Philippine Airlines, and Linea Aereopostal Venezolano were concealed through false statements made to the Export-Import Bank.

Bethlehem Steel Corporation and the Southland Corporation each established "slush funds" from which illegal payments were made in the United States to influence the outcomes of their commercial contracts.

The Bethlehem Ship Repair Yard division of Bethlehem Steel paid kickbacks to shipping line agents to direct their vessels into Bethlehem's shipyards for refitting. Padded invoices for service contracts in South and Central America were used to generate cash for a Swiss "slush fund." In 1980, the corporation pleaded guilty to violations of the Bank Secrecy Act and was fined $300,000.

The Southland Corporation, owner and franchiser of the "7-11" convenience food stores, conspired with a former New York City councilman to bribe a New York State tax official. The cash for the payoff was laundered through the councilman's escrow account and then to a bank in Toronto, Canada. These events led to the conviction of Southland and the councilman in 1984 for tax evasion and bribery conspiracies, respectively.

DEAK-PERERA

A scheme to launder $11 million by two Filipino businessmen resulted in the conviction of Deak-Perera in May 1978 for Bank Secrecy Act violations. The currency, deposited at Deak's San Francisco branch, was sent into the country in envelopes marked as business records by the two Filipinos, who operated a network of black market money exchanges. Deak-Perera willfully failed to file Bank Secrecy Act reports on the deposits, and upon conviction was fined $20,000; in addition, a Deak-Perera subsidiary was assessed $40,000 in civil penalties.[13]

INTERNATIONAL CASH FLOW

Tracing the cash flow between the United States and foreign countries provides an additional indication of the scope of the money laundering problem. In 1984, several Federal law enforcement agencies and the intelligence community participated in an analysis of the international laundering of drug profits, and made the following principal judgments:

Some $5-15 billion of the $50-75 billion in illegal drug money earned in the United States probably moves into international financial channels each year:

- More than two-thirds of the $5-15 billion is moved on behalf of foreign traffickers bringing drugs to the United States, as well as Colombians and Mexicans involved in distributing cocaine and heroin in the United States. The remainder comes from funds earned by US drug dealers and distributors.
- About one-third of the illegal drug money moves overseas in the form of currency, and much of the remainder is wired abroad after being deposited in the US banking system.
- More than two-thirds of the $5-15 billion probably passes through Colombia, or the offshore banking centers of the Caribbean Basin, mainly Panama, the Bahamas, and the Cayman Islands.[14]

Since 1980, the government has been tracking information which points to Panama as a banking center for the cocaine trade, and Hong Kong as a banking center for the heroin trade. While the international list of offshore havens is lengthy, Panama and Hong Kong deserve special attention because, in addition to being banking centers for the narcotics trade, they are also notorious transshipment and meeting points for the traffickers. In addition, they illustrate well the international aspects of the money laundering problem.

13

As part of this tracking program, the National Narcotics Intelligence Consumers Committee (NNICC), a group coordinated by the Drug Enforcement Administration (DEA) with participants from all of the Federal intelligence and narcotics agencies, recently stated:

Tracing of drug-related currency through the financial system provides valuable intelligence concerning the countries being used to launder or collect narcotics proceeds. For example, if the U.S. Federal Reserve Bank identifies a sudden "surge" of dollars from one country, this is an indication that the subject country is receiving an unusual amount of U.S. currency, possibly proceeds from narcotics activities.[15]

PANAMA

In 1982, the Department of the Treasury examined Federal Reserve receipts from the Banco Nacional de Panama, the Panamanian state bank, in an effort to quantify the amount of cocaine money accumulated in Panama. The examination revealed that the amount of U.S. dollars that the Federal Reserve receives from Banco Nacional de Panama had increased substantially in recent years. This fact indicates that the amount of cash received by the Banco Nacional de Panama from other banks or individuals in Panama also increased. Banco Nacional de Panama acts much like the Federal Reserve in that it is a clearinghouse for cash. It receives and disburses U.S. dollars to various banks in Panama, just as the Federal Reserve receives and disburses dollars to U.S. banks. The Department's review of Federal Reserve receipts from Panama shows a more than fourfold increase in the reported cash flow during 1980 to 1983.

The 1984 analysis by Federal law enforcement agencies and the intelligence community, referred to on page 13, concludes that the cash flow from Panama to the United States is the most significant recorded flow of currency that is likely to be drug money.

In comparison, some Treasury Department analysts have estimated that more than $2.2 billion in unreported cash was transported to Panama from 1980 to 1983. While this money is moved to Panama through a wide variety of methods, pilots often simply fly the unreported cash out of the United States in private aircraft.

One typical example of this practice illustrates the problem confronting law enforcement authorities. In May 1983, Mr. X[16] was apprehended as he attempted to leave a Florida airstrip in his Learjet bound for Panama. On board his plane, Customs agents found boxes containing more than $5 million in cash for which no CTRs or CMIRs had been filed. A subsequent search of Mr. X's business office revealed 30 kilograms of cocaine and an Uzi submachine gun. Information available to the DEA indicates that Mr. X not only conducted a business of moving narcotics proceeds for various traffickers, but also was preparing fraudulent U.S. tax returns. According to one estimate by law enforcement authorities, Mr. X was responsible for the movement of more than $145 million in an eight-month period, smuggling the money out of the United States to circumvent the filing of CMIRs.[17]

HONG KONG

In May 1984, the Commission began to analyze the significant heroin networks operated by criminal organizations of Southeast Asian origin. After drought years in 1979 and 1980, these Asian networks gained a gradually increasing share of the U.S. heroin market: 10% in 1981, 14% in 1982, and 19% in 1983.[18] In 1983, heroin from Southeast Asia accounted for 41% of the heroin encountered in the western United States.[19]

As with all criminal organizations, the power of these Asian groups may be measured by their ability to acquire the U.S. dollar, the international exchange standard of the underworld. To begin to measure this power, the Commission turned its attention to Hong Kong, whose role in the heroin trade has been described by the Department of State in this way:

> . . . Hong Kong is the major financial center for Southeast Asia's drug trafficking. Hong Kong-based trafficking organizations operate throughout the world. Long-standing ties between Hong Kong traffickers and sources of supply in Thailand allow Hong Kong organizations to operate on a very large scale. Large numbers of heroin trafficking ventures throughout the world are financed and controlled from Hong Kong. There is evidence that Hong Kong-based groups are involved in directing the smuggling of heroin into Europe and North America.[20]

The Commission sought not only to determine whether the volume and direction of cash flow between the United States and Hong Kong supported the Department of State's description, but also to test the value of CTRs and CMIRs as means of gathering information that could affect national policy decisions concerning initiatives to curtail international money laundering. Accordingly, the Commission interviewed law enforcement officials from Australia, Canada, Great Britain, Hong Kong, and the Netherlands (areas whose heroin-addicted population is supplied by these same Asian networks), and reviewed classified information. Bank secrecy laws in Hong Kong have historically precluded foreign law enforcement agencies from obtaining the type of information needed for full investigation of the role of Hong Kong banks as repositories for narcotics profits. The absence of currency exchange controls and a central bank in Hong Kong also hampers traditional methods of tracing the flow of funds to and from Hong Kong.

Furthermore, the "underground banking system" in Southeast Asia and Hong Kong, which exists outside the commercial banking industry, is estimated to be responsible for the transfer of a "lion's share" of the heroin money.[21] The 1984 analysis by Federal law enforcement agencies and the intelligence community described this system as follows:

> Responsible for moving most heroin money in Southeast Asia, it operates through gold shops, trading companies, and money changers, many of which are operated in various countries by members of the same Chinese family. Recordkeeping susceptible to standard audit rarely exists in this underground banking system, and coded messages, "chits," and simple telephone calls are used to transfer money from one country to another. Nonetheless the system has the ability to transfer funds from one country to another in a matter of hours, provide complete anonymity and total security for the customer, convert gold or other items into currency, and convert one currency into that of the customer's choice.

Because of the lack of information on money laundering patterns through Hong Kong, the Commission requested that the Department of the Treasury analyze, for the first time, all available cash flow data concerning Hong Kong. For 1982, the most recent year for which complete information is available, information in the possession of the Treasury Department indicates that Hong Kong is a major collection point for U.S. currency. One U.S. financial institution in Hong Kong handled approximately $700 million in U.S. currency in 1982, more than $1 billion in 1983, and more than $600 million in the first half of 1984. While about half of this currency is shipped to the United States, the balance, all in $100 bills, is shipped to other countries, principally Switzerland. Approximately 65% of the currency repatriated to this country is in $100 bills. The remainder is in smaller-denomination bills, a telltale sign of drug trafficking and money laundering. What makes these data particularly intriguing to some law enforcement authorities is that this consistent increase in U.S. currency repatriated from Hong Kong to the United States from 1982 to the first half of 1984 parallels the consistent increase in Southeast Asian heroin marketed in the United States from 1981 to 1983.

While there may be legitimate explanations accounting for the annual repatriation of hundreds of millions of dollars in smaller-denomination bills to the United States from Hong Kong, there is little, if any, evidence to support such explanations. This high volume of smaller-denomination bills exceeds the total volume of *all* currency transactions with any European country. For example, in 1982, the total shipments of U.S. currency to and from West Germany amounted to $12 million, and shipments to and from France amounted to $8.8 million. Both of these countries could be expected to have more tourist traffic and non-business contacts with the United States than does Hong Kong. Moreover, information available to the Treasury Department indicates that the flow of U.S. currency from the United States to Hong Kong is minimal when compared to the reverse flow of U.S. currency from Hong Kong. Although the Department has no information directly supporting a conclusion that the U.S. currency surplus in Hong Kong emanates from Southeast Asian drug trafficking, it is a logical explanation of this surplus.

This type of intelligence analysis can be conducted more readily in the future, if the Treasury Department implements recent plans to revise Bank Secrecy Act forms for the collection of more specific data on international currency shipments. Such analysis, if applied to other countries, would confirm the importance of the Bank Secrecy Act to strategic law enforcement planning and decisionmaking, as well as to the conduct of foreign policy in a manner that complements such law enforcement planning.

THE RESPONSE

Although organized crime has made use of money laundering techniques for some time, law enforcement agencies did not initially understand the importance of money laundering as a significant aid to organized crime. In the 1967 report of its Task Force on Organized Crime, the President's Commission on Law Enforcement and Administration of Justice did not specifically address the topic of money laundering. Indeed, there is little evidence to suggest that the national law enforcement community even recognized money laundering as a discrete activity until the end of the 1960s. Even after the enactment of the Bank Secrecy Act in 1970, and the growth in demand by narcotics traffickers for laundering schemes to conceal their enormous and increasing revenues, that recognition was slow to develop.

17

One reason for this phenomenon was that the Department of the Treasury took several years to implement the Act by establishing a system of reporting and analysis to facilitate the detection and investigation of money laundering. Today, the Treasury Department's system for assuring compliance with the Act has become so detailed that, in certain respects, it appears nearly as complex as the money laundering schemes it is intended to detect. For this reason, it is important to describe the principal features of the system in some detail.

Under the Bank Secrecy Act, the Department of the Treasury has responsibility for prescribing the types of transactions which must be reported by financial institutions and individuals, as well as the information to be detailed in such reports.[22] The Department also has oversight responsibility for monitoring and enforcing compliance with these requirements, and responsibility for assuring that information generated by the reporting requirements is disseminated in a useful form to law enforcement and regulatory agencies.[23] The Secretary of the Treasury has delegated authority for supervising compliance to the following Federal regulatory agencies:

(1) The Comptroller of the Currency (OCC), for national banks and banks in the District of Columbia;
(2) The Board of Governors of the Federal Reserve System (FRS), for all state member banks of the FRS;
(3) The Federal Home Loan Bank Board (FHLBB), for insured savings and loan institutions;
(4) The Administrator of the National Credit Union Administration (NCUA), for Federal credit unions;
(5) The Federal Deposit Insurance Corporation (FDIC), for all other federally insured banks;
(6) The Securities and Exchange Commission (SEC), for brokers and dealers in securities;
(7) The Commissioner of Customs, for reports of transport of currency across national borders;
(8) The Commissioner of the IRS, for all other financial institutions set forth in the Treasury Department's regulations.[24]

The Assistant Secretary of the Treasury for Enforcement and Operations has responsibility for coordinating the efforts of the above agencies, and in turn the agencies are required to submit periodic reports to the Assistant Secretary, with copies to the General Counsel of the Treasury Department and to the Commissioner of the IRS.[25]

The regulatory agencies charged with supervisory duties vary significantly in the number of institutions they examine, the manpower devoted to compliance examinations, and the frequency of examinations in the institutions they have been delegated to supervise.

For example, the FRS, with approximately 1,050 state member banks, has almost 900 examiners, 750 of whom are devoted to commercial bank examinations. The OCC, with responsibility for supervising compliance of roughly 4,700 national banks, has 2,000 examiners. The NCUA is charged with supervising compliance in all Federal credit unions, currently numbering over 11,000; however, the vast majority of these are state-chartered institutions with assets considerably smaller than those of competing financial institutions. Of this number nearly 5,000 are insured by the NCUA. With a total staff of about 600, the NCUA has approximately 400 examiners devoted to compliance supervision. Finally, the SEC, with responsibility for approximately 10,000 registered brokers and dealers in securities, has a staff of only 75 examiners. The SEC has delegated compliance supervision of Bank Secrecy Act provisions to the several self-regulating organizations (SRO), such as the New York Stock Exchange with 60 examiners and the National Association of Securities Dealers (NASD) with nearly 250 examiners. SEC examiners periodically conduct independent examinations and spot-check examinations of broker dealers, often with a broader focus than the SRO reviews.

The frequency of periodic examinations of financial institutions by the regulatory agencies is consistent. The FHLBB examines its 3,500 member savings and loans at least once a year, as does the NCUA. The FDIC, with over 8,900 state-chartered, Federally insured banks, examines its members at least once every twelve to eighteen months. The FRS and the OCC maintain a similar examination schedule, and each of the bank regulatory agencies can initiate more frequent inquiries as necessary at problem institutions. The SROs which supervise the compliance efforts of securities brokers and dealers routinely examine their members once a year, while the SEC examiners conduct their somewhat broader audits with less frequency.

Finally, the Examination Division of the IRS (Exams) is charged with compliance supervision of all other institutions and individuals functioning as financial institutions. While this residual category, which includes over 2,000 entities such as currency exchanges and precious metals dealers, encompasses institutions that have been, or are capable of being, used in money laundering schemes, the IRS has assigned the equivalent of only eight staff-years nationally to do routine compliance examinations.

The lack of resources in this IRS division is particularly troublesome because its agents assigned to compliance exams do not even have the authority to investigate criminal violations of the Bank Secrecy Act.

Exams only refers potential criminal violations to the Treasury Department, in the expectation that the IRS Criminal Division will undertake the actual investigation. In the last year, however, Exams reports that it has not made any referrals to the Criminal Division or to the Treasury Department of potential violations discovered during a routine compliance review.[26]

GUIDELINES FOLLOWED BY THE EXAMINERS

The supervision of financial institutions' compliance with the Bank Secrecy Act is in the hands of agencies which generally are more concerned with overseeing the safety and soundness of the financial institutions they monitor than with law enforcement.[27] With the exception of the FDIC, an examination by a regulatory agency for compliance with the Bank Secrecy Act is conducted simultaneously with the examination for general safety and soundness of the institution. The FDIC alone conducts separate compliance examinations in which state regulation, financial recordkeeping, consumer protection statutes, and Bank Secrecy Act reporting are audited for compliance.

Initially, an examiner ascertains that an institution has formal procedures to assure compliance with the Bank Secrecy Act reporting and recordkeeping requirements, and reviews an institution's list of exempt customers to determine adherence to Treasury Department regulations.[28] An examiner reviews an institution's CTRs and CMIRs to assure proper completion and filing, and conducts a limited analysis of the totals of cash shipped to and received from correspondent banks and the Federal Reserve Bank to determine whether suspect amounts of currency entered or left the institution.

If substantial irregularities are discovered an expanded review is initiated. The examiner performs an extensive review, covering a minimum of five (preferably ten or more) days of transactions in several branches of an institution, to expose potential violations of the Bank Secrecy Act.

Currency amounts shipped to and from correspondent banks or the Federal Reserve Bank are reconciled against records maintained at the branch office or currency distribution center of an institution. Examiners then look closely at branches that request large-denomination currency as a major portion of their total currency requirement, branches whose requests for large-denomination currency are significantly greater than average branch requirements, and branches with no reported exemption lists. This inspection is directed toward selection of branches for potential on-site review.

At the site, examiners review tellers' cash proof sheets for consecutive days and tellers' documentation for the selected dates, and note cash-in or cash-out transactions as well as significant drops in large-denomination bills not supported by the tellers' transactions. Examiners are alerted to currency transactions of more than $10,000 with either exempt or nonexempt customers, and consecutive transactions which total more than $10,000, in which case efforts are made to determine whether transactions were conducted by or for one depositor to circumvent reporting requirements.

Examiners scrutinize certain types of transactions carefully for suspect activity. Cashed checks, particularly multiple items cashed by the same person or a cash-out of more than $10,000 made after a split transaction, and cash deposits, savings withdrawals, or certificates of deposit redemptions in excess of $10,000, receive heightened attention. In addition, the sale of personal money orders, cashier's checks, traveler's checks, and savings bonds, as well as records of the same customer cashing any of the above instruments in unusually large amounts, are "red flags." Other unorthodox banking transactions, which have become popular as laundering techniques, are loan payments or loan proceeds in excess of $10,000 cash and transactions involving more than $10,000 cash where the bank acts as an agent for an individual.

The expanded review procedures demand that the examiner pay particular attention to details of suspect transactions and suspect teller activity. For instance, if it is a bank practice to direct all large currency transactions to specific tellers, the examiner may concentrate on the work activity of those tellers. Significant decreases in large-denomination bills (*i.e.*, fifty- and one hundred-dollar bills) not supported by teller transactions may indicate a simple money laundering technique, the exchange of smaller-denomination bills for larger-denomination bills to be carried out of the United States. Because financial institutions do not document exchanges of small-denomination bills for large ones, (except when CTRs must be completed) even this laundering technique frequently escapes review.

Examiners also pay close attention to the sale of personal money orders or official checks. Although these instruments are not necessarily in bearer form, they can be made out to cash and so have become a popular way to launder money. The purchaser is difficult to identify after the fact, and some banks do not require official approval of instruments sold for large amounts of cash. Another common scheme that examiners attempt to identify is the consecutive sale of official checks to one customer, usually in even amounts just below the threshold reporting requirement.

Finally, examiners randomly review paid instruments and check endorsements to uncover activity demonstrating a laundering pattern, such as frequent deposits at other institutions. The popularity of purchasing official negotiable instruments to further a money laundering scheme has increased for several reasons: relative anonymity of purchasers, difficulty in identifying paper trails after deposit in bank secrecy havens, widespread acceptance and ease of transferability, and the logistical ease of physically transporting a single instrument instead of suitcases full of "dirty" street bills.

Despite the thoroughness of expanded review procedures, laundering schemes frequently escape detection. It is difficult for examiners to detect illegal activity when banks and bank customers use fictitious names to conceal the true identities of individuals conducting large currency transactions. The most difficult activity for an examiner to discover, clearly, is that which occurs in connection with nonfeasance or collusion on the part of a bank employee or officer.

AGENCY REFERRALS OF NON-COMPLIANCE

After a compliance review is completed, the examining agency may elect to take administrative action against the financial institution if violations of the currency reporting and recordkeeping provisions of the Act have been discovered. For systematic failures, the action may be a follow-up letter to the institution advising it of the technical violation found. For more serious violations, the institution and the regulating agency may enter into a memorandum of understanding with correction of failures as the ultimate goal. Serious violations may cause an agency to seek a cease and desist order against an institution,[29] and in appropriate cases, to take steps to remove an officer.[30] In the case of violations discovered during examinations of securities brokers and dealers, SEC sanctions can range from a letter of caution or deficiency, to a censure of the broker/dealer, and ultimately to suspension of trading privileges.[31]

After this level of analysis, the compliance information is forwarded to the national office of the appropriate agency. The Treasury Department has issued guidelines to the agencies on the imposition of civil money penalties against financial institutions and individuals for violations of the Bank Secrecy Act. The guidelines specify that referrals for civil money penalties must be based on a determination by the regulatory agency that the violation was willful and that it has one or more of other specified characteristics, including (1) violations that are flagrant or in bad faith; (2) violations involving an insider or associate who benefited from the transactions; (3) previous violations at the institution that had resulted in a written notification from the Treasury Department or the agency; (4) imposition of a criminal penalty; (5) evidence of a pattern of violations committed with disregard for the law or consequences to the institution; (6) continuation of a violation after an institution becomes aware of it; (7) failure to cooperate with an agency to effect a resolution; (8) evidence of concealment of a violation; (9) presence or absence of a compliance program and evidence of its effectiveness; and (10) evidence that the violation concealed or facilitated illegal activity by the institution, its employees, or its customers. Once a referral is made, the Treasury Department may initiate a criminal investigation, impose a civil monetary penalty, or take no action. Regulatory agencies are required to make referrals of criminal activity, such as misappropriation of funds or bribery of an official, directly to the Department of Justice.

The regulatory agencies issue a report to the Treasury Department detailing the results of compliance examinations at six-month intervals.[32] The national offices of the various regulatory agencies accumulate information from regional offices, code it into their report to the Treasury Department, indicate all violations of the Act discovered in examinations, and, if applicable, make recommendations that civil money penalties be assessed against the institution or an individual.

IS THE ACT ADMINISTERED EFFECTIVELY?

The Commission interviewed officials at each of the regulatory agencies responsible for compliance examinations under the Bank Secrecy Act to determine what actions could be undertaken to improve effectiveness of the Act.

The agencies unanimously agreed that compliance by financial institutions has improved considerably, particularly over the last three years. This general improvement is credited to a more widespread awareness of reporting requirements, together with the well-publicized success of law enforcement projects such as Operation Greenback (discussed below). Increased awareness among examiners has resulted in the discovery of more technical violations. Moreover, the knowledge that the government utilizes reported information has had an equally dramatic effect on institutional compliance.

Several agencies voiced concerns about the periodic reports made to the Treasury Department. First, in recording the violations data, examiners are unable to distinguish between significant and technical violations. Second, the agencies unanimously stated that there is insufficient feedback from the Treasury Department after they make a referral to impose a civil money penalty against a member institution. Although the Treasury Department guidelines on the referral of cases state that a report of final action taken by the Department will be made to the referring agency, this occurs infrequently, if at all. Agency officials told the Commission that some feedback on referrals is necessary because an institution with Bank Secrecy Act compliance problems usually has other operational or supervisory problems as well. In many cases, after a referral to assess a civil money penalty has been made to the Treasury Department, agency officials said that they must rely on newspaper accounts to learn that the offending institution or bank official has been indicted by the government. While acknowledging the constraints that grand jury secrecy rules[33] and IRS rules governing disclosure of information to other agencies[34] place on the Treasury Department, the regulatory agencies expressed concern that a criminal indictment or negative publicity about bank violations can adversely affect the liquidity and safety of an institution.

Another issue raised with the Commission is that after a referral has been made to the Treasury Department, the Department frequently requests that the referring agency refrain from further examining that institution to avoid jeopardizing an ongoing criminal investigation. Lengthy periods with no feedback or progress updates from the Treasury Department can cause frustration and uncertainty for the agency. Failure to impose civil or criminal sanctions after a referral may reduce morale among agency examiners, who question their role in what generally is characterized as a law enforcement function, and may call into question the efficacy of the Bank Secrecy Act.

Figures on the number of referrals made to the Treasury Department for civil money penalties were not available from all participating agencies. The FDIC reported that, as of August 1984, three referrals for civil money penalties had been forwarded to the Treasury Department; in 1983, six; in 1981, one; and prior to 1980, three. As of July 1984, the SEC had referred four cases recommending imposition of civil money penalties against broker/dealers, as well as information about patterns of suspect cash transactions just below the $10,000 reporting requirement in certain brokerage houses. The FDIC and the SEC both report that to the best of their knowledge, no penalties have been imposed on the referred institutions.

The Treasury Department has informed the Commission that since the enactment of the Bank Secrecy Act in 1970 it has assessed civil money penalties against four financial institutions. In 1978, Deak & Co. of California was fined $40,000 for 377 violations of the Bank Secrecy Act which occurred from 1972 to 1976. In 1981, Republic National Bank of New York was fined $20,000 for CMIR violations on 1,768 shipments of currency, and National Republic Bank of Chicago was fined $9,000 for 25 CTR violations occurring from 1978 to 1980. In 1983, First National Bank in Louisiana was fined $35,000 for violating CTR requirements 35 times from December 1979 through July 1982.[35] No civil penalty has ever been levied against an individual bank employee for violations of the Act.

When financial institutions file CTRs in accordance with current Treasury Department regulations and procedures, it may take the Treasury Department six to eight weeks or longer for the data on the CTRs to be processed and made ready for analysis at the Treasury Financial Law Enforcement Center (TFLEC). Treasury Department regulations currently permit financial institutions to file a CTR as late as 15 days after the day on which the transaction occurred. Thereafter, the IRS must process all CTR data at its facility in Ogden, Utah, and transport the input data to a U.S. Customs Service office in San Diego, California, before transporting the data to TFLEC at headquarters. TFLEC analysts and Treasury Department officials may then require additional time for review and analysis of the CTR data.

If the Treasury Department concludes, after review and analysis of CTR or CMIR data, that those data suggest the existence of a money laundering scheme in a particular region of the country, the Department's regulations sharply limit its authority to transfer CTR or CMIR data to other agencies outside the Department.[36] While these regulations are arguably consistent with the spirit of the Bank Secrecy Act, they effectively preclude any transfer of data to any other agency outside the Treasury Department unless that agency has already begun a formal investigation on an offense to which such data might be relevant. This procedure does not take into account the fact that agencies outside the Treasury Department would find these data to be of substantial importance in determining whether they should open an investigation. For example, neither the FBI nor the DEA can check to see whether the head of a family of La Cosa Nostra or another criminal organization is engaging in large cash transactions unless that person is already the subject of an active investigation.

When supervisory agencies conduct routine audits, their examiner's could also be substantially aided if they had a list from the Treasury Department of all CTRs and CMIRs that have been submitted by a particular institution at the time the audit begins. Such a list would permit auditors to discover discrepancies when they review the financial institutions' own file of CTRs and CMIRs. In the Great American Bank case (see discussion at page 39), for example, just this type of abuse was discovered, in part because the FDIC examiner assigned to the bank had been furnished a list of CTR filings received by IRS prior to the examination, and in part because Great American Bank officials had inaccurately and fraudulently completed the forms that were on file. This comparative procedure might require more examiner time, but it is an effective process to determine the veracity of an institution's reporting.

In addition, at the time of the audit, examiners usually do not have a list of customers who have been exempted from the Act's reporting requirements. While regulations specify that all exemptions granted must be kept in a centralized list, the list is not made available to auditors until they request it from the financial institution.

OPERATION GREENBACK

Once criminal cash flow has been detected, the Bank Secrecy Act has proven to be an effective way to prosecute some launderers. The government's concerted law enforcement program called Operation Greenback provides an example.

Operation Greenback is a Treasury Department program to identify and investigate individuals involved in laundering large amounts of currency generated from drug trafficking through financial institutions in Florida. The IRS and the Customs Service are the major participants, with assistance from the DEA. Operation Greenback was initiated in July 1980 after the Treasury Department discovered an unusual surplus of currency in Florida financial institutions.

The Federal Reserve Banks in Miami and Jacksonville received a surplus of $3.3 billion in currency from financial institutions in Florida during 1978. In contrast, the other 35 Federal Reserve Banks shipped out currency which exceeded the currency received from financial institutions in their regions by $3.5 billion. In addition, the unusual surplus in Florida had increased from $921 million in 1974, and was climbing to an expected $6 billion by 1980.

The targets identified to date include attorneys, accountants, money brokers, money couriers, bankers, and banks involved in facilitating the flow of drug money through financial institutions and across U.S. borders to foreign countries. Operation Greenback has documented $2.6 billion in U.S. currency that has been laundered through 16 narcotics organizations. There have been 164 arrests, 211 indictments, 63 convictions, $38.5 million in seized currency, $7.5 million in seized property, and $117 million in IRS jeopardy and termination assessments.[37]

In many cities across the country, there have been significant Bank Secrecy Act prosecutions as well. In 35 major cities, financial investigative task forces using the "Greenback" concept of cooperation among IRS, Customs and the Justice Department have been established. The effectiveness of Bank Secrecy Act prosecutions is evident from these statistics:

- In fiscal year 1983, 425 individuals were indicted, resulting in 239 convictions to date.

- In the first half of fiscal year 1984, another 587 individuals have been indicted and 154 convicted.
- The numbers indicted in fiscal years 1983 and 1984 to date exceed the total number of individuals indicted for Bank Secrecy Act violations during the previous ten fiscal years.

The effectiveness of such prosecutions, however, is limited because Federal statutes do not grant law enforcement authorities use of all the investigative tools they need. Because participants in money laundering schemes frequently travel to different areas within the United States or aboard, and must communicate over long distances with the criminals whose funds they are laundering, telephones, telexes, and other forms of electronic communications—as in the Orozco case (see discussion at page 35)—play a vital role in facilitating and maintaining such schemes. At present, however, a criminal violation of the Act does not constitute an offense on which the Justice Department can predicate an application for court-authorized electronic surveillance.

In addition, the criminal provisions of the Act do not explicitly prohibit attempts to violate the CMIR reporting requirements. As a result, some Federal courts have taken substantially different views of whether a person's failure to fill out a CMIR by the time that person has checked baggage and headed toward the departure area, or has stepped onto the jetport preparing to board the airplane after the flight has been called for boarding, constitutes a violation of the CMIR requirements.[38]

Finally, as noted earlier, the civil and criminal penalties imposed by the Act are far too lenient to discourage money laundering. When the Treasury Department can impose a civil penalty of no more than $1,000 per violation, and Federal courts can sentence defendants to no more than one year in prison and $1,000 per violation (absent a showing of a pattern of such violations), the risk to the launderer is negligible when contrasted with the seemingly limitless financial potential of laundering.

CASE STUDIES

The flow of narcotics proceeds can be best detected in the early stages of the laundering process (*e.g.*, at the initial transactions with domestic financial institutions). Accordingly, this section highlights money laundering cases that involve various types of domestic financial institutions, ranging from a full-service bank to a small savings and loan association in a New York suburb, to the U.S. branch of a foreign bank, and to an international currency exchange.

The studies also demonstrate the geographic diversity of money laundering schemes. Each case was selected because it illustrates some aspect of domestic money laundering schemes which the government has investigated. In some cases employees of the financial institution played an integral role in the conduct of the scheme; in other cases the institution was used as an unwitting vehicle to conduct the criminal activity.

In analyzing these cases, the Commission examined the role played by the institution's employees who dealt directly with the money launderer; the mechanisms that were in place within the institution to prevent or detect officer or employee corruption; the point, if any, at which employees became suspicious enough to question the launderer's transaction; and whether officials reported their suspicions about certain customers or their transactions to law enforcement agencies. The Commission also analyzed the role played by the government agency responsible for assessing the institution's compliance with currency reporting requirements. The Commission conducted interviews with key personnel and government auditors and subpoenaed documents to explore these issues more fully.

Some observations can be made from the case studies. First, when a criminal and an officer or employee, collude to launder funds, ways to thwart the reporting requirements will be devised and usually will succeed. Detection of insider collusion schemes is the most difficult and the most costly to the government. Even though money launderers have corrupted, or attempted to corrupt, officials and employees of financial institutions when conducting their laundering activities, the Bank Secrecy Act provides neither civil nor criminal penalties for such conduct, and the penalties under the existing Federal criminal statutes for bribery of bank officials are far too lenient. Under sections 215 and 216 of Title 18, the maximum criminal penalties for bribery of officers, directors, employees, agents, or attorneys for FDIC-insured banks, Federal land banks, and small business investment companies are $5,000, one year's imprisonment, or both.

Second, many of the institution's employees involved in these cases adopted a posture of deliberate indifference to suspicious transactions or customers. Because of their longstanding concern for their customers' privacy, financial institutions typically have been unwilling to question customers closely about their financial transactions, or to notify law enforcement authorities of their suspicions concerning a customer unless the evidence of illegal activity is clear and unambiguous. In some instances, financial institutions have told customers suspected of money laundering that their business was no longer welcome, but they did not inform the authorities of their suspicions.[39]

Third, even when financial institutions have been willing to notify Federal authorities of suspicious transactions, the Right to Financial Privacy Act, which closely confines the authority of Federal agencies to obtain the records of financial institutions' customers, provides that certain categories of financial institutions (*e.g.*, banks and savings and loan associations) may notify a government authority only that they have "information which may be relevant to a possible violation of any statute or regulation."[40] Because this provision does not itself authorize a financial institution to disclose the information that it believes to be relevant to the violation of law, the financial institution could be subjected to substantial civil liability, including actual and punitive damages and attorney's fees, if it voluntarily disclosed any information in a customer's financial record without first receiving either the customer's authorization or a subpoena, summons, or search warrant. Under these circumstances, many financial institutions have been reluctant to risk incurring civil penalties for cooperating with law enforcement.

Fourth, in some instances, officials of financial institutions that have been contacted by law enforcement authorities for information concerning the accounts of customers have notified the customers of the authorities' interest, even when it was clear to those officials that violations of the law were being investigated. Such notification can obstruct the conduct of criminal investigations. As Justice Thurgood Marshall recently wrote in a unanimous opinion of the United States Supreme Court in *Securities and Exchange Commission* v. *Jerry T. O'Brien, Inc.*:[41]

> [Notice to third parties] would substantially increase the ability of persons who have something to hide to impede legitimate investigations by [an agency]. A target given notice of every subpoena

30

issued to third parties would be able to discourage the recipients from complying, and then further delay disclosure of damaging information by seeking intervention in all enforcement actions brought by the [agency]. More seriously, the understanding of the progress of an ... inquiry that would flow from knowledge of which persons had received subpoenas would enable an unscrupulous target to destroy or alter documents, intimidate witnesses, or transfer ... funds so that they could not be reached by the Government.

Moreover, United States Attorney for the Central District of California, Robert C. Bonner, stated to the Commission that this problem of notification "is pervasive and has become an impediment in conducting major white collar and narcotics financial investigations. There have already been reported incidents of such disclosures in pending cases in this district and elsewhere."[42]

In a number of cases, financial institutions have also asserted that under their state financial privacy statutes, their failure to disclose to a customer that they have received a Federal grand jury subpoena for that customer's records would subject them to potential civil or criminal liability under state law. A few judicial decisions in recent years have held that under the Supremacy Clause of the United States Constitution, any provision of state law purportedly requiring a financial institution to notify the customer must give way to provisions of Federal law with which the state law is in conflict.[43] To date, however, neither Congress nor the courts have definitively resolved this issue.

On some occasions, financial institutions that have been suspicious about particular customers and their transactions have not known which law enforcement agency to contact, or have contacted one or more agencies without seeing any of the agencies actively investigate the matter. In addition to the law enforcement agencies, such as the FBI and the DEA, that have infrequently participated in various money laundering investigations, as previously noted, eight agencies have responsibility for assuring compliance with the Bank Secrecy Act. While the overall responsibility for coordinating the procedures and efforts of these agencies rests with the Treasury Department, no one agency within the Treasury Department has been designated as the principal contact and investigative entity for pursuing Bank Secrecy Act violations.

THE PIZZA CONNECTION

On April 9, 1984, thirty-eight individuals were charged in an indictment filed in the Southern District of New York, as a result of a Federal investigation into heroin trafficking and money laundering in this country and in Europe by various elements of La Cosa Nostra, including the Bonanno crime family. Informally known as the ''Pizza Connection,'' the network was one of the largest importers of heroin into the United States, and used pizza parlors throughout this country to distribute heroin smuggled in from Southeast Asia's Golden Triangle via Sicily.

Law enforcement authorities have generally recognized that members of La Cosa Nostra and the Italian Mafia have been involved in heroin trafficking since the late 1930s and early 1940s. According to the 1984 analysis by Federal law enforcement agencies and the intelligence community,

> Heroin has always been the drug commodity preferred by [the Mafia]. Much of the heroin handled by American [Mafia] figures has been processed in laboratories under the control of their Italian counterparts in Sicily. A downpayment, ranging from a small fraction to 100 percent of the delivered price, reportedly is required in advance of shipment. Out of a total take of some $2.5 billion from heroin sales, US [Mafia] families probably send up to $1 billion annually in payments to suppliers in Sicily. There is considerable probability that a substantial share of US profits is reinvested directly within the [Mafia] economic empire or laundered domestically for legitimate investment purposes, although some US family drug money finds its way into Swiss bank accounts.

The ''Pizza Connection'' case provided new evidence of the extent to which elements of La Cosa Nostra and the Italian Mafia have jointly participated in narcotics trafficking and the laundering of narcotics proceeds through financial institutions in the United States.

According to a criminal complaint filed in the case on April 19, 1984, Joseph Bonanno, born in Sicily in 1905, emigrated to the United States in 1925 and became active in the New York La Cosa Nostra. Bonanno is believed to be a major figure in the planning of the heroin network operated by organized crime in the United States, Sicily, and elsewhere.

Bonanno attended three meetings to discuss, among other matters, the Bonanno family's role in heroin trafficking. In October 1956, Bonanno met at Binghamton, New York, with his ''underboss,'' Giovanni Bonventre, and his consigliere (counselor), Carmine ''Lilo'' Galante. The second meeting occurred in late October or early November 1957, in Palermo, Sicily. In addition to Bonanno and Galante, other known La Cosa Nostra members attended this meeting, including Gaspare Maggadino, John Di Bella and ''Lucky'' Luciano.[44] The third meeting took place on November 14, 1957, at Apalachin, New York and included fifty-seven La Cosa Nostra leaders and associates in addition to Bonanno. Bonanno disappeared in 1964, and was not observed again by law enforcement authorities until 1966, when he settled in Tucson, Arizona, where he presently resides.

The heroin importation network relied upon a faction of the Bonanno crime family headed by Salvatore Catalano to distribute the heroin in this country. In turn, the heroin business of this Bonanno crime faction was tied directly to organized criminal groups in Sicily, the rest of Italy, Switzerland, Spain, and Brazil. Direct evidence of the existence of the network was first obtained in 1980 when couriers were observed transferring enormous amounts of cash through investment houses and banks in New York City to Italy and Switzerland. Tens of millions of dollars derived from heroin sales in this country were transferred overseas in this fashion, apparently in violation of the Bank Secrecy Act.

According to the complaint, the function of the couriers was to transport cash out of the United States. Generally, the cash was in $5, $10, and $20 denominations, or "street money," and was transported out of the country by private jet to Bermuda, by commodity account transfers between New York City and Switzerland, and various other means. These funds were then channeled from Switzerland or Bermuda back to the narcotics sources in Italy. The money was used to pay for the raw opium converted into heroin in the Sicilian laboratories, to finance additional laboratories, and otherwise to support and profit the overall network of heroin trafficking.

One of the couriers for this laundering operation was Franco Della Torre, a Swiss resident. In March 1982, Della Torre deposited slightly more than $1 million in $5, $10, and $20 bills in the "Traex" account at the Manhattan office of the brokerage firm Merrill Lynch Pierce Fenner & Smith. Thereafter, Della Torre made 4 additional cash deposits totaling $3.9 million in the "Traex" account at Merrill Lynch in late March and mid-April 1982.

In making large cash deposits at Merrill Lynch, Della Torre's practice was to request that security personnel accompany him from his hotel to Merrill Lynch offices. After several such deposits, security employees determined that Della Torre's funds could not be afforded proper security, and arrangements were made to escort the money from Della Torre's hotel directly to Bankers Trust, where Merrill Lynch maintained accounts. A Merrill Lynch security official, noting the suspicious nature of transactions and Della Torre's reluctance to enter the "money room" at Bankers Trust due to the presence of surveillance cameras, contacted the Merrill Lynch manager in Zurich, Switzerland, regarding the legitimacy of the "Traex" account. In spite of assurances that the account was in order, Merrill Lynch closed the account in April 1982, whereupon Della Torre moved his laundering operation to the Manhattan office of the brokerage firm E. F. Hutton & Company.

From April 27 through July 2, 1982, Della Torre made 7 cash deposits totaling $5.2 million in a "Traex" account at E. F. Hutton. Between July 6 and September 27, 1982, Della Torre made 11 similar cash deposits totaling $8.25 million in the account of "Acacias Development Corporation" at E. F. Hutton in Manhattan.

Of the total $18.3 million deposited by Della Torre in the Merrill Lynch "Traex" account and the two E. F. Hutton accounts, an undetermined portion was transferred to a "P.G.K. Holding" account at E. F. Hutton. According to Swiss authorities, P.G.K. Holding was listed as an importer and exporter of precious gems. Records of this account reflect that nearly $13 million was eventually transferred out of the United States to pay for commodity futures contracts in Switzerland.

Commission interviews established that in April 1982, an E. F. Hutton senior vice-president directed an employee to arrange for large cash deposits at Bankers Trust for a then unidentified client. Della Torre arrived at Bankers Trust for the first such arranged deposit with two gym bags filled with small-denomination bills, excused himself from the counting room, and returned a short time later with an additional bag filled with money. After two deposits totaling nearly $4 million were made, Bankers Trust refused to accept further transactions of this nature with Hutton, ostensibly because of an inability to free employees for counting money. In reality, Banker's Trust officials were concerned about the legitimacy of the cash deposited, and one official shared those concerns with an E. F. Hutton official. The Hutton official responded that E. F. Hutton was making the deposit and that Bankers Trust would not be liable for anything. When interviewed by the Commission, this E. F. Hutton official stated that he did not recall this conversation with the Bankers Trust official.

Hutton officials subsequently arranged for Della Torre's cash deposits into the "Traex" and "Acacias" accounts at other New York financial institutions, and established security protection from Della Torre's hotel to the depository institution on three separate occasions. The Hutton employees responsible for the delivery of Della Torre's cash, when interviewed by the Commission, stated that no efforts were made to contact their legal department regarding Della Torre's deposits despite the admittedly highly unusual nature of the transactions.

In addition, on October 5, 1982, E. F. Hutton was served with a Federal grand jury subpoena regarding Della Torre and the "Traex" and "Acacias" accounts. Hutton officials, including Hutton's general counsel, promptly notified an associate of Della Torre in Switzerland of the subpoena, despite requests by the government that no such disclosure be made. On October 10, 1982, P.G.K. Holding deregistered itself in Zurich and moved to Zug, Switzerland. Della Torre made no further deposits.

According to the complaint, information from confidential sources indicates that other indicted members of the heroin network were involved in money laundering activities. Adriano Corti, a member of the Catalano faction, identified himself to a European financier as a principal of COOP Finance in Switzerland. Corti explained that he had a client, a "prominent industrialist," in New York City, who was interested in transferring $5 million to $6 million cash from the United States to Switzerland. Between October 20 and November 21, 1980, approximately $1.78 million in cash was shipped to Switzerland from deliveries arranged by Corti in New York City. Another confidential source observed approximately $2 million in cash denominations of $5, $10, and $20 bills being delivered in New York City at Corti's direction between October and December 1980. This source stated that the cash deliveries were made by automobile by several members of the Catalano faction who transported the cash in gym bags, suitcases, and cardboard boxes. Yet another confidential source indicated that another member of the heroin network, Phillip Salamone, customarily transported currency from New Jersey to a location in New York State, where another individual smuggled the currency across the border into Canada. The ultimate destination of the money was believed to be Sicily.

The complaint states that agents believe that between October 1980 and February 1981, approximately $6.9 million in cash was collected and transported from New York City to banks in Bermuda and Switzerland. Together with amounts deposited by Della Torre, authorities believe that the heroin network laundered at least $25.4 million between October 1980 and September 1982.

THE EDUARDO OROZCO CASE

Over a four-year period ending in November 1982, Eduardo Orozco and a number of associates deposited approximately $151 million in cash in eighteen bank and currency exchange accounts, and transferred it to accounts elsewhere in the United States, Panama, the Bahamas, and the Cayman Islands. While much of the money came from Colombian cocaine dealers, Orozco's laundering customers also included Sicilian heroin traffickers of La Cosa Nostra, including Antonio Turano, who was found murdered in New York City in March 1983.

A joint Customs, DEA, and IRS investigation was initiated in 1981 when Orozco's attorney became suspicious that the numerous bank accounts which he had established and managed on behalf of Orozco were being used to launder illegal proceeds. The attorney apparently knew Orozco as a Colombian importer and exporter of coffee, but became concerned about the frequency, manner, and size of deposits which were being made into these accounts. The attorney introduced an undercover DEA agent, acting as a Citibank official, to Orozco, who quickly took the agent into his confidence.

In the three months that followed, the undercover DEA agent was given a desk at Citibank and established an account through which Orozco laundered almost $3.5 million, with approximately one-third of that amount transferred to accounts in Panama, another one-third to other foreign bank accounts, and the remainder to domestic U.S. banks. Another account which the undercover DEA agent established for Orozco was in the name of a Panamanian corporation; the account holder was listed as an individual other than Orozco, to avoid identifying Orozco with the account.

Orozco was so pleased with the undercover DEA agent's assistance that he offered to pay the agent a commission of 1/10th of 1% of all cash deposited into the account. Later, he increased the commission when the agent agreed to place Orozco's account on a bank exemption list, thereby eliminating the completion of CTRs for that account. Orozco made a profit because he charged his customers a percentage fee to launder their money and another fee to convert the laundered dollars into the specific South American currency requested. Early in the sting operation, Orozco stated to the government agent that the money was generated by a laundering network he headed on behalf of South American coffee merchants. Several months later, however, Orozco admitted that the money originated ''60% to 70%'' from drug trafficking. Orozco took care to insulate himself, he explained to the undercover agent, by dealing only with intermediaries who delivered the money to him, thereby creating a buffer between himself and the drug dealers.

Seven months after his initial meeting with Orozco, the undercover DEA agent had been paid $13,000 in commissions for the $4 million deposited into the accounts. Although Orozco severed his connection with the agent once he suspected the agent's true identity, the government's investigation continued with further analysis of Orozco's accounts and the use of the first court-authorized telex intercept order. Records recovered after the arrest of Orozco and members of his organization showed that telex messages were sent to his counterparts in Colombia with detailed information reporting the receipt and transfer of monies along with the specific banks and accounts involved.

On June 30, 1983, Orozco was found guilty of conspiracy to violate drug laws and was sentenced to eight years in prison and was fined $1 million.

Orozco used several methods to conceal the source and amounts of currency in his operation:

- Small-denomination bills were converted into larger-denomination bills.
- Amounts just under $10,000 were deposited, many times using couriers, to avoid the filing of CTRs.
- Shell corporate entities were set up, and deposits into these accounts were made through inter-corporate transfers, adding another level of insulation.
- False "bills of lading" were used to substantiate the deposit and transfer of funds among export/import companies.

Orozco used eleven banks, each receiving a portion of the total $151 million which he laundered. One of the institutions involved accepted fifty-three cash deposits from an "R. Cespedes," an Orozco accomplice, although he in fact made only four deposits himself. The Orozco case grew in magnitude because most of the financial institutions he used failed to verify the depositor's identity.

More than two-thirds of the money moved by Orozco—approximately $97 million—went through his accounts with Deak-Perera, a currency exchange based in New York City. The Deak-Perera account was used between November 1980 and March 1982. Orozco opened this account in the name of Dual International (Interdual), which purportedly was a retail currency exchange. Although Interdual claimed that it purchased foreign currency and checks in exchange for U.S. currency, in dealing with Deak-Perera Interdual deposited only U.S. currency. In fewer than sixteen months, this account received 232 cash deposits totaling almost $97 million. These deposits were often carried in cardboard boxes to the Deak-Perera New York City branch. One series of deposits in October 1981 involved a $3.4 million deposit, followed two days later by a $999,000 deposit, followed one day later by a $537,000 deposit, followed within five days by a $879,000 deposit, and three days afterward by a $1.5 million deposit—all in cash. Customarily, the deposits remained only a few days before they were transferred to other accounts in U.S. cities, Panama, the Bahamas, and the Cayman Islands.

In an interview with DEA agents, Deak-Perera officials admitted that Deak-Perera employees did not verify the identity of individuals opening accounts, and that Deak-Perera did not require the account holder to open the account in person or to present himself at the Deak-Perera branch to transact business. At its March 14, 1984 hearing on money laundering in New York City, the Commission sought the voluntary cooperation of Deak-Perera's chairman, Nicholas Deak, in providing additional details about the Orozco case and responding to questions from Commission members.

Deak refused to testify voluntarily, and the Commission was unable at that time to compel his testimony. Previously, in an interview with the Commission, Deak failed to explain how millions of dollars could have been laundered through Deak-Perera. Instead, he professed not to know the threshold amount for reporting and asked whether the money laundered through Deak-Perera was *only* drug money. Deak also stated that he was too far removed from the problem to be of any assistance to the Commission.

Four of the New York banks used by Orozco—Chase Manhattan Bank, Marine Midland Bank, Irving Trust Company, and Credit Suisse—terminated his privileges and refused to accept his business at some point in the course of his scheme. In interviews with knowledgeable bank officials, the Commission found that with the exception of Marine Midland Bank, none of the banks took active steps to notify law enforcement officials about Orozco's suspicious transactions:

- Orozco opened an account for the Calypso Travel Agency at Chase Manhattan Bank, with a $60,000 cash deposit. Thereafter, Chase Manhattan accepted two other cash deposits, of $40,000 and $50,000, to the account. Calypso Travel initially had been placed on Chase's exemption list; it was removed from that list because of a ''change in bank policy'' which, an employee told the Commission, was unrelated to suspicions about Orozco's transactions.
- Credit Suisse allowed an Orozco nominee, Alvarez Segura, to make a cash deposit of $57,795, which was followed the next day by a cash deposit of $249,000. While the bank eventually closed this account, it never contacted law enforcement officials to report any concerns. A review of the bank's daily cash deposit records readily revealed that these two Orozco-related deposits were far larger than any others logged for the same time period.
- Irving Trust Company allowed Orozco's attorney to maintain an account for his client and to deposit large sums of cash on behalf of Orozco almost without question. Officials of Irving Trust have since informed the Commission that under Irving Trust's current ''personal banker'' system, immediate steps would be taken to close accounts of any customers suspected of criminal activity.
- Marine Midland Bank's branch in Jamaica, Queens accepted a cash deposit of $830,000, which Orozco's couriers had brought into the bank in a bag. Orozco's attorney, who was a well-known customer at the bank, called the branch manager to alert him to the arrival of the $830,000. Although the branch initially accepted

the deposit and completed a CTR, the branch manager became concerned about it and called the bank's associate counsel for instructions on how to handle the transaction.

The counsel instructed the manager to put a hold on the Orozco account, to ship the cash directly to the Federal Reserve with a note that it be kept segregated and inspected for counterfeits, and to prepare and express-mail the CTR (on which a bank employee had independently noted suspicion about the transaction) to the IRS's processing center for CTRs in Ogden, Utah. When interviewed by the Commission, the bank's associate counsel said that he gave these instructions because he felt that this transaction would be of "interest to law enforcement."

The next day, Orozco's attorney again asked the bank to accept a $1 million cash deposit. The branch manager was then instructed by his superiors to close the account. In spite of a request from the FBI that Marine Midland keep the account open and accept the deposits from Orozco's attorney, the account was closed.

Representatives of these four banks unanimously noted that, with the benefit of hindsight, suspicious transactions such as Orozco's would cause the bank to close the customer's account "without question." All of the representatives said that depositors need proper identification and references. All, however, were uncertain about whether they could or would report suspicions to law enforcement authorities, and were unclear which Federal agency should be contacted.

GREAT AMERICAN BANK

As a result of Operation Greenback, a Federal grand jury indicted the Great American Bank of Dade County, Florida (GAB) and three employees, including the vice president of the installment loan department, a loan officer, and the head teller. The indictments, returned as a series from December 1982 through April 1984, charged that the bank laundered more than $94 million from January 1980 through February 1981, and willfully failed to file 406 CTRs during that period. In addition, the bank's depositors—three separate narcotics organizations—were charged in three companion indictments. All defendants who are not fugitives have pleaded guilty to various charges, including failure to file CTR reports and conspiracy to provide money laundering services for narcotics-related organizations.

The money laundering schemes effected through GAB included agreements between the narcotics trafficking organizations and the vice-president of GAB, Lionel Paytuvi. The traffickers agreed to maintain large balances in their accounts, and the bank and certain personnel would receive a fee for processing and counting large currency deposits. The fee was divided equally between the bank, Paytuvi, and Carlos Nunez, a loan officer, who then divided his share with the head teller, Elaine Kemp. Carlos Nunez and the head teller also agreed not to file CTRs for deposits of currency in excess of $10,000; in addition, Nunez issued cashier's checks disguised as loan proceeds to the drug dealers, and processed their money through foreign and interstate accounts.

One of the narcotics trafficking organizations, holding an account under the name Interfil, made cash deposits of over $71 million from January 1980 through February 1981, with average deposits in excess of $250,000 daily. Interfil did no legitimate business, and existed only as a GAB account and a front for cocaine and marijuana sales as well as narcotics money laundering services. Cash proceeds were taken to GAB in boxes and suitcases, for which GAB imposed a processing fee of 0.5%, later increased to 0.75%; Interfil maintained an average daily balance of $500,000-$600,000. GAB routinely issued cashier's checks two or three days following the cash deposits, enabling the bank to realize further profits until the checks were negotiated.

From April 1980 through December 1980, GAB maintained another account for "Luis Rondon" in which currency deposits in excess of $9 million were made. The "Rondon" account was a nominee account for Carlos Piedrahita, a known narcotics supplier from Colombia and partner of Isaac Kattan. The 1984 analysis by Federal law enforcement agencies and the intelligence community noted that Kattan, who was eventually indicted for his role in the GAB scheme, had pursued a criminal career that

> probably constitutes a prototype of the traditional relationship between Colombian drug traffickers and money exchangers. With his links to drug money movement already established, Kattan probably was one of the principals involved in the shift of cocaine money laundering from New York City to Miami in the 1970s. He subsequently functioned virtually as "Chancellor of the Exchequer" for at least one major cocaine-trafficking organization—a degree of involvement that does not appear to have been duplicated, at least in the United States, since his arrest and the impoundment of his records.

In return for maintaining a large balance and the customary fee for accepting deposits, GAB agreed not to file CTRs for deposits in excess of $10,000. In fact, the bank's loan officer did file CTRs at various times, falsely listing GAB as the owner of the deposited money, and kept copies of both filed and unfiled CTR reports in the event of examination by bank regulators or law enforcement authorities.

In early February 1981, GAB officials met with Kattan and agreed to process a $3 million cash deposit by issuing cashier's checks to various Kattan accounts at the Bank of Miami in exchange for a $20,000 fee, paid in advance, to GAB. Later, at GAB's insistence, Kattan opened a checking account in the name of "Currency Exchange Corporation," and made large daily currency deposits totaling more than $6 million in February 1981. The entire $6 million in cash were the proceeds of sales of narcotics, smuggled primarily from Colombia.

Kattan's operation involved the cash deposits of large sums of narcotics proceeds by Kattan or his couriers into his "Currency Exchange Corporation" account, where it was transferred via cashier's check, wire transfer, or check to the Bank of Miami, where Kattan held an account in the name of "Sofisa." GAB assisted in the money laundering scheme by routinely falsifying names of remitters on Kattan's cashier's checks, as well as failing to file the required CTR.

After a series of transactions through foreign tax havens, the U.S. funds would then appear as assets of Kattan's Colombian travel agency, which was also a front for Kattan's Colombian black market money exchange. Kattan could then pay Colombian narcotics traffickers in Colombian pesos, as well as finance the transportation of narcotics from Colombia to the United States. In many instances, currency never left the United States because of Kattan's large source of pesos from his black market money exchange, which he acquired by transferring various U.S. bank checks rather than actual U.S. currency.

For the money deposited during February 1981, Kattan paid Nunez fees totaling $47,000. Kattan and his couriers always did business openly at GAB, bringing bags and boxes directly to the lobby where the money was counted.

Upon being introduced to the principal individuals of the "Rondon" and "Interfil" accounts, one GAB officer expressed his pleasure with their average daily balances and voiced appreciation for their business. After an FDIC examination of GAB in September 1980, in which an FDIC examiner discovered twelve CTRs showing GAB as the party bringing cash into the bank, a GAB officer instructed the vice president, Paytuvi, not to issue cashier's checks out of installment loans, but to issue the checks from another department. At no time did other bank officers question Paytuvi, Nunez, or Kemp whether CTRs were being filed. Officers and employees alike treated the drug traffickers as valued customers, despite the frequent appearance of counterfeit bills in the cash deposits.

On April 16, 1984, the bank pleaded guilty to four counts of failure to file CTRs and was fined $500,000.

DEAK-PERERA AND ISAAC KATTAN

Isaac Kattan's laundering activities were not limited to GAB. In mid-1978, at the request of the Treasury Department, the IRS began a CTR compliance examination of Deak-Perera (New York) covering the period January 1, 1977 through June 30, 1978. The IRS examiner handling the case soon discovered suspicious financial activity in accounts belonging to Kattan. Later, in 1982, the IRS agent spotted the Interdual account used by Orozco to launder more than $97 million.

In 1977 and 1978, Kattan had maintained Deak-Perera accounts in New York in the name of "Jose Vega." IRS's investigation disclosed that Deak-Perera employees had seen Kattan's passport and knew that he maintained his accounts under false names—a fact that Kattan readily admitted when he was made available to the IRS agency by a Deak-Perera accountant for an interview in February 1979. Nonetheless, Deak-Perera filed 27 CTRs for deposits—which were in fact made by Kattan—to the "Jose Vega" account.

The IRS audit also indicated that in 1978, Deak-Perera filed 58 false CTRs with respect to Kattan's account. In addition, the audit revealed that in 1978 alone, there were 53 separate Kattan deposits which were split among several code name accounts in amounts less than $10,000 for which no report was filed.

When notified that Deak-Perera was the subject of an investigation, officials of Deak-Perera insisted that their company had taken corrective action to ensure that CTR violations would not take place in the future because of a tightening of internal controls. In March 1982, Deak-Perera was informed that the IRS agent would conduct a subsequent examination covering the three-month period from October to December 1981, to test Deak's claim. By mid-May 1982, the IRS agent discovered the Interdual account through which Orozco was then laundering approximately $97 million.

The IRS compliance examination revealed that, in the period under review, 1,266 CTRs totaling nearly $230 million were not filed by Deak-Perera. In addition, the Customs Service identified 356 transportations of currency totaling $47.5 million in which Deak-Perera failed to file the required CMIRs.

The Commission has learned that the Treasury Department has advised Deak-Perera that it may be assessed a $572,000 civil penalty for reporting violations associated with the Orozco and Kattan cases. If this civil penalty becomes final, it will amount to five times the total of all civil penalties ever imposed by the Secretary of the Treasury under the Bank Secrecy Act.

PAN AMERICAN INTERNATIONAL BANK

This Las Vegas bank, its chairman of the board, its president, and a bank cashier were indicted in 1983 on charges that they conspired, made false statements, and failed to file CTRs in an effort to conceal almost $400,000.

In September 1982, an undercover IRS agent, posing as a corrupt Mexican official, opened a checking account at the Pan American International Bank. The bank's new accounts clerk counseled him not to deposit more than $10,000 because the bank would have to report the transaction to the IRS.

One month later, the undercover agent returned to the bank, this time to meet with the bank chairman. He was told that currency deposits from Latin Americans would not be reported to the government because the bank was interested in attracting business. During the next three months, the agent deposited $295,000 and was in turn given $100,000 in cash by the chairman and the president. As promised, the bank officers did not report any of these transactions. To further their scheme, the bank officers tutored the undercover agent on a story he could use if bank examiners questioned his accounts.

In February 1983, the FDIC made its first routine examination of the bank, which had opened for business eighteen months earlier. Although the FDIC was unaware of the IRS's undercover activities, it received an anonymous tip about suspicious transactions which began with an individual carrying a satchel of cash into the bank. Locating the particular transaction, the FDIC examiner mistakenly believed that he had uncovered a loan fraud perpetrated by the bank's top-ranking officers. The examiner located the bank's copy of a CTR that it had filled out for the transaction, but he was unaware that the bank had never filed the form with the government. The FDIC then sent a letter to the United States Attorney in Las Vegas setting forth possible criminal violations by the bank.

The bank pleaded guilty in 1984 to charges of conspiracy to fail to file CTRs, as part of a pattern of illegal activity involving transactions of more than $100,000 in a twelve-month period, as well as conspiracy

43

to submit a false, fictitious, or fraudulent statement to the IRS, and was fined $25,000. The bank cashier also pleaded guilty to the above charges after testifying for the government, and was placed on probation. The vice-chairman of the board, convicted on all three counts after a trial by jury, is currently awaiting sentencing; the chairman was acquitted.

LIU CHONG HING BANK

From July 1982 until April 22, 1983, four individuals associated with the Liu Chong Hing (LCH) Bank (headquartered in Hong Kong with a branch in San Francisco) agreed to launder $1.5 million in supposed ''narcotics proceeds'' for two undercover IRS agents.

The agents used an informant to obtain an introduction to Aaron Lee, owner of the Canada-Asia Finance Group, Ltd. of Vancouver, British Columbia. Representing themselves as narcotics traffickers, the agents said that they were looking for a way to launder their drug proceeds and asked Lee for his assistance in arranging a laundering scheme through Hong Kong banks. Lee said that he could arrange for large amounts of cash to be moved through U.S. branches of foreign banks, and advised that his services would cost $10,000 and 5% of each month's deposits.

After the agents accepted his plan, Lee traveled to Hong Kong and made preliminary arrangements with LCH Bank vice president So Kwong Sing. A bank account in the name of a fictitious company, controlled by Lee, was set up so that funds in the United States could be transferred to it. Another account was created to be used and controlled by the agents to receive some of the funds derived from the currency deposits. Lee returned to the United States, met with the agents, and escorted them to a San Francisco branch vice president, who accepted a deposit of $442,500 for which he did not file a CTR.

Two weeks later, the agents were given an address in Hong Kong by the branch official and were instructed to meet with LCH Bank vice president So and a Hong Kong accountant. In Hong Kong, the agents were told by So and the accountant to divide their deposits into specified smaller amounts, to vary their pattern of deposits and to ''build in some odd figures so that the whole lot could not add up to a round sum''—all to circumvent the currency reporting requirements. The agents were given completed deposit slips of eleven different persons, on the LCH Bank accounts specifying amounts of currency to be deposited at the San Francisco branch. After these funds were deposited, they were to be transferred among other bank accounts at the Hong Kong LCH bank, until they ultimately were deposited into an account under the control of the two IRS agents. To avoid any uncertainty, the agents were given a diagram to help them better understand the flow of funds between dummy and control accounts.

At this stage of the operation Aaron Lee had been removed by the agents, who now dealt directly with the bank officials. Under a new agreement, the agents were to pay 1% of their monthly deposits to the bankers for their "services," and in turn were to receive a 1% commission for any new "customers" they introduced to the Bank.

Four individuals were indicted in September 1983 on conspiracy and false statement charges, as well as currency transaction violations relating to $500,000 that had been laundered.

Aaron Lee was convicted, although he testified against his co-conspirators as a government witness, and has just completed his six-month sentence. The San Francisco branch official was acquitted but So, the vice president in Hong Kong, was convicted after trial. The case against the Hong Kong accountant is pending.

GARFIELD BANK

In July 1981, a Federal grand jury in Los Angeles indicted the Garfield Bank and seven individuals, including the Bank's chairman and two former vice presidents, for the willful failure to file CTRs and conspiracy to defraud the government. Twenty-nine transactions, ranging in size from $36,020 to $491,790 and totaling more than $3.3 million, were tracked through the bank over a two-year period. Concealment of narcotics proceeds was the apparent motive for directing funds through the bank.

Nathan Markowitz, an attorney who provided laundering services for narcotics traffickers, established "nominee" accounts at Garfield, foreign corporations in Panama and Liberia, trusts at the Bank of Bermuda, and sham corporations in California. Large amounts of currency were deposited into various accounts over which Markowitz maintained control. This money was then wire-transferred to trusts at the Bank of Bermuda or was used to purchase cashier's checks at the Garfield Bank for Markowitz's clients. To conceal the nature, and disguise the amounts, of currency flowing from offshore corporations to the United States, Markowitz used false documents to give the appearance of legitimate, non-taxable income for his clients.

The key to the success of the laundering operation in this case was the complicity of bank officials who willingly and knowingly failed to file CTRs. The chairman and president of the bank, John A. Gabriel, was charged with "willfully causing the bank not to file" CTRs for Markowitz's transactions. Gabriel permitted his private office to be used

45

for counting the narcotics money. Bank vice presidents William Jebb and Warren Zacovic personally assisted Markowitz and his associates in converting their illegal narcotics proceeds, and approved the non-filing of CTRs.

Undercover IRS agents, posing as narcotics traffickers, infiltrated the scheme in 1980. During a meeting with one agent, vice president Zacovic instructed him to "get a letter on file that you will be making deposits over $10,000 periodically" so that the deposits would be considered usual and consistent, thereby exempting the depositor (agent) from currency reporting requirements.

Vice president Jebb allegedly received 2% of the total amounts deposited, for his active role in assuring that transaction reports for Markowitz's clients were not filed. When a deposit was "accidentally" made at a bank branch where a conscientious employee insisted on filling out a CTR, Markowitz allegedly instructed Jebb to "sit on the report."

After he was named an unindicted co-conspirator and agreed to cooperate with the investigation, Nathan Markowitz was murdered in April 1981; authorities believe that the murder was an unrelated act committed by another of Markowitz's drug trafficking clients.

On December 15, 1981, the defendants were found guilty on all counts. As a result of its successful prosecution of the Garfield Bank and its president and officers, the government may collect approximately $2.3 million in fines, penalties, back taxes, and interest.

MASPETH SAVINGS & LOAN ASSOCIATION

In June 1981, Giuseppe Gallina, Vincent Beltempo, Giuseppe Aiello, and Barbara Walberg were tried in New York for their involvement in smuggling heroin from Palermo, Sicily into the United States. According to Federal investigators the smuggling venture had its roots in the "Golden Crescent" of the Near East, where morphine base was produced and smuggled into Sicily and then converted into heroin. From Sicily, the heroin was transported to mainland Italy and then flown to New York. In this venture, thirty-two pounds of heroin were smuggled into the United States: sixteen pounds were seized, and the remainder apparently found its way into this country.

When Gallina was arrested in connection with this drug investigation, he had in his possession mortgage papers from the Maspeth Federal Savings & Loan Association concerning property he co-owned. The DEA agent who arrested Gallina went to the bank in Queens, New York, and interviewed the vice president of Maspeth Federal. The agent obtained a subpoena for Gallina's records and his accounts at Maspeth Federal. The vice president said that since 1979 Gallina and his family had transacted cash business with the institution in excess of $400,000. Many individual deposits were in excess of $10,000. On several occasions, the person making the transaction would simply exchange cash for a teller's check. In January 1981, Gallina came into the savings and loan with $50,000 in cash in a small airline bag. He exchanged it for two teller's checks worth $25,000 each. Gallina then used this money as partial payment for a house he purchased. He also allegedly used several members of his family, in return for cash, to obtain cashier's checks for him.

During DEA's review of the institution's records for these accounts, it became evident that employees were ignorant of CTR requirements. They were unaware that a CTR form was to be completed and sent to the Department of the Treasury for each cash transaction in excess of $10,000. Maspeth Federal, however, maintained a handwritten "log" of all transactions over $10,000 since 1957, and this log preserved the transactional record law enforcement officials needed to reconstruct the evidence for the successful prosecution of the defendants.

DEA advised Maspeth Federal's vice president that the institution was in violation of Federal law, and forwarded that information to the IRS Criminal Division in New York. The IRS opened an investigation of Maspeth Federal and began interviewing employees, eventually subpoenaing Federal Home Loan Bank examination reports. A year later the case was closed without prejudice. After consultation with prosecutors, it was determined that (1) there was no intent by the institution or its employees to violate the reporting requirements; (2) it could not be proven that the institution had been officially notified, warned, or criticized about its failure to report currency transactions as a result of regulatory examinations; and (3) the institution's own records for all cash transactions above $10,000 were not only complete and equivalent to CTR requirements, but predated Federal reporting requirements.

Defendants Gallina, Beltempo, and Walberg were found guilty; Aiello was acquitted on all counts. Another defendant pleaded guilty, while three other individuals remain fugitives.

PEOPLE'S LIBERTY BANK

In February 1984, Luis Pinto, a Colombian native, was sentenced to ten years in prison and fined $525,000 for his part in an international scheme to launder profits from cocaine sales. Federal authorities charged Pinto with laundering sums in excess of $11 million between August

1981 and August 1983, as part of his operation to make drug proceeds appear to have been gained legitimately.

Pinto transacted business primarily for a drug ring centered in Colombia. In addition to People's Liberty Bank in Covington, Kentucky, Pinto used banks in Panama, Miami, and Canada. He did business at the central office of People's Liberty Bank and six branch offices located throughout Kentucky. Pinto deposited large sums of currency, often close to $300,000 at a time, in either his personal account or various business accounts at the central branch of People's Liberty Bank. According to authorities, Pinto then made withdrawals in the form of bank drafts and cashier's checks, usually in amounts of $10,000. Pinto frequently made withdrawals of $10,000 from several different branch locations in a single day in attempts to circumvent CTR requirements. Cashier's checks and other payments from the accounts eventually found their way to Colombia, or reappeared as ostensibly legitimate proceeds of shell businesses that Pinto owned or operated in the Covington area.

People's Liberty Bank never notified local or Federal law enforcement officials of suspicious banking activities by Pinto. When large cash deposits were made into his accounts at the central branch offices, bank officials routinely found counterfeit bills, generally regarded as an indication of the presence of drug-related money.

CHEMICAL BANK

In February 1977, Chemical Bank, the sixth-largest commercial bank in the United States with 244 branches in the New York City area, was the first financial institution to be indicted under the Bank Secrecy Act. Chemical Bank and three of its officers were charged with laundering money for several narcotics dealers, one of whom was Frank Lucas, a La Cosa Nostra associate. The bank officials exchanged smaller-denomination bills for larger ones. The bank failed to report more than $8.5 million in more than 500 cash transactions, some of which included individual cash exchanges ranging from $10,000 to $250,000.

Chemical Bank pleaded guilty to more than 200 misdemeanors in exchange for the court's dismissal of felony charges, and was fined more than $200,000 plus court costs. When the IRS checked CTR filings by Chemical Bank one year after its indictment, filings had increased 950% from the prior period. In March 1977, two of the officers pleaded guilty to failure to report as income the cash payments they received in exchange for their laundering services.

Thomas Spinelli, one of the convicted Chemical Bank officers, was a branch manager during the period from 1971 to 1974 when he laundered money for narcotics dealers. Spinelli, who had been a manager at Chemical Bank since 1961, obtained the cooperation of fifteen other bank employees and officers under the pretext that he was helping his cousin, a bookmaker, "wash" money. Those employees received a share of the 1% to 1-1/4% commission that Spinelli received for his services. The cooperation of other branch managers, head tellers, and assistant managers was essential because of the large volume of cash arriving regularly at Spinelli's branch.

In a deposition taken by the Commission on August 28, 1984, Spinelli described the delivery of cash from drug traffickers in paper bags, suitcases, and attache cases. No bank employee ever refused Spinelli's request for assistance in his illegal scheme, perhaps because, as Spinelli said, his "associates viewed the Government's reporting requirements as an infringement on the people who were known member(s) of the community and who may have to make a large transaction from time to time."

Ironically, Spinelli had assisted Chemical Bank with the preparation of its operations manual. He told the Commission that operational flaws enabled his scheme to go undetected long after it should have been discovered. Spinelli noted that a branch manager's routine check of the head teller's sheet should have highlighted the huge volume of large-denomination bills going out of the bank. However, no procedures were in effect during Spinelli's tenure as branch manager to require branch managers to make such checks.

The successful prosecution of Chemical Bank and its officers prompted the bank to implement policies and procedures to ensure that Spinelli's scheme could not be repeated. One such policy, "know your customer," advises employees that it is the policy of Chemical Bank "to do business only with individuals, businesses, and other entities whose reputations are sound." Furthermore, the employee who establishes the customer relationship is charged with the responsibility to determine that customer's character and reputation. Corporate policy directs the employee to notify an appropriate senior vice president, division head, or subsidiary head immediately when it appears that the bank's reputation and that of the customer are not compatible for any reason. Finally, inquiries regarding suspicions concerning a customer's reputation are to be directed to the Investigation Department. Information on customers whose business the bank rejects is routed to the Investigation Department, to be disseminated and used.

CONCLUSIONS AND RECOMMENDATIONS

CONCLUSIONS

1. Every financial institution, including banks, savings and loan associations, currency exchanges, and casinos, should assume that it is a potential target for use by organized crime in money laundering schemes. Existing policies and internal controls have frequently proven inadequate to prevent criminals from using the services of these institutions.

2. While the Bank Secrecy Act is the principal basis for Federal law enforcement agencies to detect, investigate, and prosecute money laundering activities by members and affiliates of organized criminal groups, and while the Act has proven to be a potent weapon against money laundering activities, several factors have limited its effectiveness:

a. When a financial institution, the Treasury Department, or other Federal law enforcement agency suspects that one of the institution's customers may be engaging in money laundering, the Federal agencies are likely to confirm their suspicions with reliable information only after substantial, if not indefinite, delay. This delay is the result of several phenomena: the reticence of financial institutions to inform law enforcement authorities of suspicious transactions; the strictures that state and Federal law have placed, or are perceived to have placed, on the disclosure of financial institutions' records; the lack of information about which agency to contact concerning possible violations of law; the time required for processing and analyzing CTRs; and the restrictions placed on the Treasury Department in transferring CTR and CMIR data to other Federal agencies.

b. To date, the principal responsibility for monitoring and investigating money laundering has rested solely on the Department of the Treasury and its components. Other law enforcement agencies that could bring substantial investigative experience and resources to bear on the problem have not been able to share some of that responsibility with the Treasury Department, because those agencies lack jurisdiction to investigate much of the laundering-related

51

activity that has been criminalized under the Bank Secrecy Act or other Federal statutes.

c. Because auditing of financial institutions by Federal bank supervisory examiners has resulted in the discovery and referral of only a few money laundering cases, the Federal Government cannot rely on the audit function of these agencies as the primary means of detecting and investigating money laundering schemes. Such agencies are better suited to provide ancillary support for the Treasury Department's efforts to ensure compliance with the Bank Secrecy Act.

d. Under the Act, as currently administered, Federal agencies lack some investigative techniques and resources that they need to deal effectively with money laundering schemes: authority to conduct electronic surveillance in accordance with the provisions of Title III for Bank Secrecy Act violations; insufficient numbers of FBI, DEA, and IRS agents to investigate violations of the Act and other money laundering-related violations; and the general availability of such documents as exemption lists and lists of CTRs and CMIRs filed with the Treasury Department for bank examiners in advance of an audit in which they are expected to ensure compliance with the Act.

e. The Act does not provide sufficient authority to prosecute and to penalize money laundering effectively. At present, the civil and criminal penalties for willful violations of the Act are not stringent enough to accomplish their intended purpose, and the felony provisions of the Act can be applied only in extremely limited situations where multiple violations constitute a "pattern of illegal activity." Moreover, even though money launderers have corrupted, or attempted to corrupt, officials and employees of numerous financial institutions in conducting their laundering activities, the Act provides neither civil nor criminal penalties for such conduct, and the penalties under the existing Federal criminal statute on bribery of bank officials are far too lenient. Finally, the absence of an attempt provision in the Act has created substantial difficulties for law enforcement agencies and courts in determining when conduct by a money launderer constitutes a completed offense under the Act.

RECOMMENDATIONS

In light of the foregoing facts and conclusions, the Commission believes that the following recommendations are worthy of detailed further examination:

A. Voluntary Guidelines for Financial Institutions

The Commission has formulated voluntary guidelines which financial institutions can adopt in response to the problem of money laundering. They were developed after interviews with officials of financial institutions, reviews of several bank internal policy manuals, and observance of routine daily operations in a wide variety of financial institutions. The proposals take into account distinctions between individual institutions, such as their size, number of branches, and amount of commercial activity. In some instances, proposals are drawn from procedures already implemented in banks and considered by the Commission to be a model for other institutions. However, these proposals are not intended to be a policy manual or "how-to" guide, but are intended to alert responsible officials to possible shortcomings in their institutions' internal policies.

1. Party Responsible for CTR Completion

In reviewing the internal procedures of several banks, the Commission found that there are significant differences between methods of completion and filing of CTRs. In some circumstances the teller to whom cash is presented completes the form; in others, a specific teller is designated to handle large currency transactions and complete forms; in yet others, the branch manager is responsible for completion of the form and filing the report with the central bank office. In most procedures, however, only one employee is required to sign the CTR.

The branch manager or assistant manager should be ultimately responsible for completion of the CTR, and be required to countersign the CTR. This procedure should guarantee the thoroughness of information on the form, and ensure that the report is properly channeled within the institution prior to its filing with the IRS. In addition, institutions may increase their ability to detect suspect financial activity by designating a "risk management officer"—a mid-level manager who is ultimately responsible for activity within a specific sector of the bank's operation—to review all completed and countersigned CTRs.

2. Training for Officers and Employees

The Commission found that the amount of time devoted to teller training on Bank Secrecy Act compliance is usually less than one hour, with tellers instructed only in the most elementary requirements of the law and regulations.

Tellers should receive more extensive training, not only in the requirements of the regulations, but in the features common to money laundering schemes and the purposes and importance of the Bank Secrecy

Act. Minimal training and preparation should expose the teller to potential situations where illegally obtained cash is brought into the bank, and to actions which are characteristic of money laundering schemes, such as "spreading" and "splitting" transactions in a single day.

In particular, tellers and the officers or employees who directly supervise them should be specifically instructed to recognize certain characteristics of customers who may be engaging in money laundering:

- An individual who makes large cash deposits when the business of that individual or his corporation is not of a type known to generate substantial amounts of cash;
- A person whose individual or corporate accounts show virtually no normal business-related banking activities and who uses those accounts primarily as a temporary repository for funds ultimately transferred to foreign bank accounts;
- Corporate accounts whose transactions, both deposits and withdrawals, are dominated by cash rather than by forms commonly used in commercial transactions, such as checks, loan proceeds, letters of credit, or banker's acceptances;
- A customer who provides minimal or fictitious information, or information that the financial institution cannot readily verify, concerning such matters as property ownership, credit history, or sources of income, particularly when the provision of such information would make the customer eligible for credit lines or additional banking services that a legitimate customer would find valuable;
- An individual engaging in numerous cash transactions, or purchasing cashier's checks, in amounts just below the $10,000 threshold for completion of CTRs;
- A customer who maintains an inordinately large number of accounts not commensurate with the type of business purportedly being conducted, and/or who engages in an inordinately large number of fund transfers between these accounts;
- A customer who makes regular large cash deposits or withdrawals associated with wire transfer to, from, or through narcotics source or transit countries, or countries whose secrecy laws have been known to facilitate the laundering of the proceeds of narcotics trafficking; and
- In the case of a currency exchange, a customer who uses the exchange's services to wire cash without changing the form of the currency (*e.g.*, U.S.-dollar-to-U.S.-dollar transfers).

While these characteristics may also be observed in the context of wholly legitimate transactions, they can provide financial institutions with at least some guidance on the steps that they can take to discourage money laundering.

3. Internal Auditing Function

Many financial institutions, including banks and savings and loan associations, have internal audit groups to examine their routine functions and activities. However, no institution reviewed by the Commission has an audit unit devoted solely to Bank Secrecy Act compliance, and the enormous number of technical violations discovered during government compliance checks clearly indicates that far too little attention is given to this area.

To aid in their self-review for compliance with the Act, financial institutions should implement an internal clearinghouse for all CTRs and CMIRs generated in branch commercial activity. Such an internal function would enable management to review compliance efforts at an early stage.

4. Exemption Lists

When customers wish to be exempted from the Act's reporting requirements, financial institutions should perform background investigations which are as thorough as those performed on loan applicants. Special attention to the customer's business needs and the proposed upper range of exempt currency transactions is a necessity. If an exemption is to be granted to a customer, this decision should be approved by at least two officers of the financial institution, reducing opportunities to corrupt officials in furtherance of a laundering scheme.

5. Fiduciaries

Internal auditors should give particular attention to activities that frequently evade cursory review, such as the purchase and cashing of large-denomination cashier's checks and deposits or exchange of large amounts of currency by a person in an agency or fiduciary relationship with the principal or account holder. Because this practice has occurred in documented money laundering schemes, review of such transactions should be expanded to reveal patterns of suspicious activity.

6. Electronic Data Processing

The Department of the Treasury and the financial community should undertake a joint study to determine the feasibility and cost of on-site electronic data processing of Bank Secrecy Act reporting forms. The current processing system creates a significant lag between the time of a suspicious financial transaction and the time at which this information is available to investigators.

7. Notification to Law Enforcement Agencies

Financial institutions should establish a formal policy that encourages their officers and employees to report promptly to the appropriate law enforcement agencies all transactions suspected of involvement with money laundering. Such a policy should recognize the need of law enforcement agencies to receive such reports as soon as possible during or after the transactions, as well as the duty of the institution to act in conformity with Federal and state law governing the financial privacy of its customers. In implementing such a policy, each financial institution should provide specific guidelines to its tellers and branch supervisors for identifying such transactions.

B. Administrative Recommendations

1. To increase substantially the costs and difficulties associated with the conduct of money laundering, and to deter money launderers in the United States from using foreign countries so freely for money laundering, the Department of the Treasury should determine which countries are most likely to be repositories for significant amounts of laundered money, by combining a country-by-country analysis of CTRs, CMIRs, and Foreign Bank Account Reports (FBARs) with investigative information obtained from various Federal agencies. Thereafter, the Department of Justice should expand on its use of Financial Task Forces and develop teams of United States Attorneys, other Department of Justice attorneys, and investigative agencies to coordinate their investigations and prosecutions of money launderers on a country-by-country basis, to target the foreign countries most heavily used for money laundering from the United States.

2. To increase the effectiveness with which the IRS can review financial transactions for compliance with the Bank Secrecy Act, and to ensure that financial institutions have a specific Federal agency to contact if they become aware of violations of the Bank Secrecy Act, the Secretary of the Treasury (through the IRS) should be given substantial additional personnel, devote those personnel (including both Revenue Agents and Special Agents) and resources (including civil summons power) to the IRS office that handles Bank Secrecy Act compliance, and designate that office as the initial contact for financial institutions.

3. To complement the efforts of the Department of the Treasury to assure compliance with the Bank Secrecy Act, and to facilitate the efforts of the FBI and the DEA to investigate other money laundering-related violations within their respective jurisdictions, the Attorney General (through the FBI and the DEA) should be given substantial additional personnel and devote those personnel to investigations of such violations.

4. To reduce the time that is required to process and analyze CTR data, the Secretary of the Treasury should consolidate the processing of such data into a single location.

5. To expedite the process by which financial institutions can inform law enforcement agencies of specific violations of the reporting requirements under the Bank Secrecy Act, the Secretary of the Treasury and financial institutions should coordinate the implementation of a procedure whereby a financial institution can make a special standardized notation on any CTR or CMIR that it believes involves a questionable transaction, mail that CTR or CMIR, as appropriate, to the IRS or Customs office responsible for inputting such data, and telephone a particular office (such as the IRS compliance office) to alert it to the contents of the CTR or CMIR. Such a procedure would in no way conflict with the provisions of the Right to Financial Privacy Act, and can quickly call the attention of law enforcement agencies to a possible money laundering scheme, as the Orozco case demonstrates.

6. To facilitate review for Bank Secrecy Act compliance during audits of financial institutions, the Secretary of the Treasury should arrange for the generation of exemption lists compiled by financial institutions, as well as lists of CTRs and CMIRs that have been received by the Department of the Treasury from particular financial institutions, and for the transmission of those lists to bank examiners or other auditors in advance of their audits of those institutions.

7. To discourage officials or employees of a financial institution from abusing that institution's authority to exempt customers from the requirements of the Bank Secrecy Act, the Secretary of the Treasury should amend the Department of the Treasury's regulations under the Bank Secrecy Act to establish the following procedure: (1) the customer requesting the exemption would be required to complete and sign a sworn statement (falsification of which would violate 18 U.S.C. §1001), on a form provided by the Department, that sets forth all of the information concerning the exemption that the financial institution is currently required to maintain, as well as the information that the customer has provided to the institution in support of the request for the exemption; (2) the financial institution would be required to submit the form to the

Department within seven working days after the customer has completed and signed the form.

8. To minimize the possibility, in situations where a law enforcement agency has requested information from a financial institution concerning a customer, that disclosure of the agency's request might result in the destruction of evidence or other impediments to the agency's investigation, the agency should request that the financial institution not disclose the agency's request for information to the customer until the agency has provided the customer with the notice required under the Right to Financial Privacy Act. In those instances where the agency has obtained a judicial delay in notice under section 1106(c) or 1109(a) of the Right to Financial Privacy Act, and an official or employee of the financial institution notifies the customer of the agency's request for information during the pendency of that delay, the Department of Justice should consider criminal prosecution of that official or employee under Chapter 73 of Title 18, United States Code (concerning obstruction of justice), if the notification to the customer results in one of the circumstances described in section 1109(a)(3) of the Right to Financial Privacy Act.

9. To discourage the use of casinos by criminals as conduits for money laundering, and to subject casinos, where appropriate, to the reporting and recordkeeping requirements of the Bank Secrecy Act, the Secretary of the Treasury should amend the regulations under the Act to include casinos in the definition of "financial institutions." (While the Commission endorses such an inclusion, as the Department of the Treasury has proposed in its recent notice of proposed rulemaking, the Commission offers no additional comment at this time on any other aspect of that notice.)

10. To improve communications between the Department of the Treasury and bank supervisory agencies concerning Bank Secrecy Act compliance, and to encourage those agencies in their efforts to ensure such compliance, the Department of the Treasury should formally notify a bank supervisory agency that has referred a case to the Department for investigation of possible criminal violations of the Act, if the referral results in the filing of an indictment or information. In appropriate cases, the Department of the Treasury should also formally express its appreciation to any employee or unit of the bank supervisory agency whose work significantly contributed to the referral.

C. Legislative Recommendations

(Note: As this report went to print, the House of Representatives, on October 11, 1984, passed legislation, H.J. Res. 648, containing,

58

either in whole or in part, recommendations 4, 6, 7, 9, and 10, marked with asterisks on the following pages.)

1. To permit financial institutions to cooperate more actively and regularly with Federal law enforcement agencies in providing information concerning ongoing money laundering schemes, Congress should amend the Right to Financial Privacy Act. Such an amendment should permit those institutions not only to notify the agencies that they have information which may be relevant to a violation of law, but also to disclose a sufficient amount of such information to permit the agencies to determine whether a formal investigation is warranted and how such an investigation should proceed. Such an amendment could be drafted so that all subsequent disclosures of information in customers' financial records could be made only in conformity with the provisions of the Right to Financial Privacy Act. (See Appendix.)

2. To clarify the law concerning Federal agencies' rights of access under state law to the financial records of financial institutions' customers, Congress should also amend the Right to Financial Privacy Act to preempt the provisions of any state constitution, statute, regulation, or judicial decision that create a more stringent standard for financial institutions' disclosures to Federal agencies than the Act does. (See Appendix.)

3. To ensure that financial institutions will not inadvertently render themselves subject to private damage actions under the Right to Financial Privacy Act for disclosing information to law enforcement agencies concerning violations of law, or for failing to notify customers of such disclosures, Congress should amend the Right to Financial Privacy Act. Such an amendment should permit an institution to raise as a defense that it had disclosed the information in a good-faith belief that it may be relevant to a possible violation of a statute or regulation. (See Appendix.)

4.* To increase the incentive for officials or employees of financial institutions or other persons to inform Federal agencies that money laundering is taking place at a particular institution, Congress should add a provision to the Bank Secrecy Act that would permit the Secretary of the Treasury to give rewards for information leading to penalties under the Bank Secrecy Act. (See Appendix.)

5. To facilitate the process by which the Department of the Treasury may transfer information in reports filed under the Bank Secrecy Act to other Federal agencies, Congress should amend the Bank Secrecy Act. Such an amendment would permit the Secretary of the Treasury to

transfer information in those reports not only when the head of an agency specifically requests such information in connection with a formal open investigation by that agency, but also when the Secretary has reason to believe that making such information available to an agency, even if not specifically requested by that agency, would further or facilitate the exercise of the Secretary's supervisory or regulatory powers under the Bank Secrecy Act. (See Appendix.)

6.* To facilitate the investigation of money laundering schemes by making possible the interception of telephone calls, telexes, and other forms of wire or oral communication in accordance with the provisions of Title III of the Omnibus Crime Control and Safe Streets Act of 1968, Congress should amend Title III to include the criminal provisions of the Bank Secrecy Act as a predicate for the issuance of judicial orders authorizing such interceptions. (See Appendix.)

7.* To increase the effectiveness of the civil penalty in the Bank Secrecy Act, Congress should amend the Act to increase the maximum civil penalty under the Act from $1,000 to $10,000, except for cases involving a willful violation of any reporting requirements, in which the fine should equal the amount of the monetary instruments. (See Appendix.) In determining the amount of the penalty to be levied against a domestic financial institution, or a partner, director, officer, or employee thereof, for a willful violation of the Act, the Secretary of the Treasury should take into account whether the institution has adopted formal procedures for ensuring compliance with the Act, as well as the scope and detail of such procedures and the vigor with which the institution applies and enforces them. In addition, the Secretary should arrange for public announcements, through the office of public information at the Department of the Treasury, whenever the Department institutes or concludes a proceeding for the imposition of a civil penalty under the Act.

8. To increase the effectiveness of the criminal penalties in the Bank Secrecy Act, Congress should amend the Act to (1) increase the maximum criminal fine from $1,000 in all cases to the greater of $250,000 or twice the amount of the monetary instruments for the first such offense, and to the greater of $1,000,000 or five times the amount of the monetary instruments for each subsequent offense; (2) increase the maximum term of imprisonment from one year in all cases to five years for the first such offense, and to ten years for each subsequent offense; and (3) make the enhanced criminal penalties applicable in cases where the person committing the offense has done so as part of a pattern of illegal activities that include, but that are not limited to, violations of the Act or the regulations thereunder. (See Appendix.)

9.* To discourage and to penalize more heavily the corruption of officers or employees of financial institutions by money launderers, Congress should amend Sections 215 and 216 of Title 18 so that the penalty for the use of bribery or graft concerning financial officials can be increased from a misdemeanor to a felony. (See Appendix.)

10.* To facilitate the apprehension of money launderers who seek to transport large amounts of currency from the United States without completing and submitting a CMIR, Congress should amend the Bank Secrecy Act to make such attempts to transport a violation of the Act. (See Appendix.)

* * *

11. Each of the foregoing recommendations addresses some feature of the current enforcement of the Bank Secrecy Act and related statutes and regulations. Each, if put into effect, can do much to enhance the capabilities of law enforcement agencies to cope with the increasingly sophisticated techniques of money launderers, without encroaching upon constitutionally guaranteed rights.

Yet these recommendations also have a common defect: neither individually nor collectively do they strike directly at the activities in which money launderers engage. One fact that is often overlooked in assessing the effectiveness of the Bank Secrecy Act is that while the Act has clearly enabled law enforcement agencies to detect money laundering activities more readily, it addresses the problem of money laundering indirectly by subjecting the money launderer to financial penalties or imprisonment only if he or she willfully violates the Act. As a result, the money launderer who complies with the recordkeeping and reporting requirements of the Act and the regulations by completing CTRs and other forms, as money launderers have frequently done in the past, can operate with virtual impunity, unless and until it can be proved that the launderer has violated another Federal statute.

The effects of money laundering, however, are too pernicious and too widespread to justify the belief that a highly limited scheme of Federal regulation, standing alone, will suffice to deal with the problem. The complex and sometimes ingenious techniques of professional money launderers make it possible for drug traffickers and other criminals to conduct illegal activities with substantial confidence that the profits from such activities can be safeguarded from detection and seizure by law enforcement agencies.

Moreover, money laundering invariably has a deleterious effect upon the financial community. By corrupting officials and employees of financial institutions in furtherance of laundering schemes, money launderers

61

undermine the integrity of those institutions and, if discovered by law enforcement agencies, can vitiate the reputations of those institutions for soundness and prudent judgment. Even if a financial institution is unwittingly made a conduit for laundering, the mere fact that money launderers saw fit to use that institution may seriously affect the public's perception of the institution.

These facts clearly indicate that if financial institutions are to be adequately protected from abuse of their services by money launderers, and if law enforcement agencies are to deal more effectively with the problem of money laundering, the Federal Government must strike directly at the heart of the problem by making the use of financial institutions by money launderers a criminal offense.

Under the Commerce Clause of the United States Constitution, Congress clearly has the power to make the transmission of monetary instruments for purposes of money laundering a separate criminal offense. In *California Bankers Association* v. *Shultz*, which upheld the constitutionality of the Bank Secrecy Act, the United States Supreme Court stated:

> The plenary authority of Congress over both interstate and foreign commerce is not open to dispute, and that body was not limited to any one particular approach to effectuate its concern that negotiable instruments moving in the channels of that commerce were significantly aiding criminal enterprise. . . . Congress could have closed the channels of commerce entirely to negotiable instruments, had it thought that so drastic a solution were warranted; it could have made the transmission of the proceeds of any criminal activity by negotiable instruments in interstate or foreign commerce a separate criminal offense. (Emphasis supplied.)[45]

For these reasons, Congress should amend Title 18 of the United States Code to add a new section that would explicitly prohibit the conduct of transactions involving monetary instruments when the person conducting the transaction, or causing it to be conducted, intends to promote, manage, or otherwise further unlawful activities that typically are conducted by organized criminal groups, or knows that the monetary instruments represent income or proceeds from such activities. Such legislation would give Federal law enforcement agents clearly defined authority to investigate money laundering activities from the customer's side of the teller's window—to deal with money launderers and their couriers from the time they enter a financial institution.[46]

The Commission has prepared draft legislation that would address this issue, as well as an explanation of its principal provisions. (See Appendix.) This legislation, together with the preceding recommendations, should make it possible for the Federal Government to develop a fully coordinated national strategy to combat money laundering. If money laundering is the keystone of organized crime, these recommendations can provide the financial community and law enforcement authorities with the tools needed to dislodge that keystone, and thereby to cause irreparable damage to the operations of organized crime.

THE FINANCIAL INSTITUTIONS
PROTECTION ACT

A Recommendation to the President

and the Attorney General of the United States

From the President's Commission on Organized Crime

October 1984

THE FINANCIAL INSTITUTIONS PROTECTION ACT

TABLE OF CONTENTS

A BILL

Be it enacted by the Senate and House of Representatives of the United States of America in Congress assembled, That this Act may be cited as the "Financial Institutions Protection Act"

TITLE I — SERIOUS NON-VIOLENT OFFENSES

PART A - MONEY LAUNDERING

Sec. 101. (a) Chapter 95 of title 18, United States Code, is amended by adding the following new section:

"§1956. Laundering of monetary instruments

"(a) Whoever conducts or causes to be conducted a transaction or series of transactions involving one or more monetary instruments in, through, or by a financial institution which is engaged in, or the activities of which affect, interstate commerce, or attempts so to do,—
    "(1) with intent to promote, manage, establish, carry on, or facilitate the promotion, management, establishment, or carrying on, of any unlawful activity; or
    "(2) with knowledge or reason to know that such monetary instruments represent income derived, directly or indirectly, from any unlawful activity, or the proceeds of such income,
"shall be fined not more than $250,000 or twice the value of the monetary instruments, whichever is greater, or imprisoned not more than five years, or both, for the first such offense, and shall be fined not more than $1,000,000 or five times the value of the monetary instruments, whichever is greater, or imprisoned not more than ten years, or both, for each such offense thereafter.
"(b) As used in this section—
    "(1) the term 'conducts' includes, but is not limited to, initiating, concluding, or participating in conducting, initiating, or concluding a transaction;
    "(2) the term 'transaction' includes, but is not limited to, a deposit, withdrawal, transfer between accounts, exchange of currency, loan, extension of credit, purchase or sale of any stock, bond, certificate of deposit, or other monetary instrument, or any other payment, transfer, or delivery by, through, or to a financial institution, by whatever means effected;

"(3) the term 'monetary instruments' means monetary instruments as defined in section 203(1) of the Currency and Foreign Transactions Reporting Act, as revised (31 U.S.C. §5312(a)(3));

"(4) the term 'financial institution' means financial institution as defined in section 203(e) of the Currency and Foreign Transactions Reporting Act, as revised (31 U.S.C. §5312(a)(2)); and

"(5) the term 'unlawful activity' means any act or acts constituting—

"(A) a pattern of racketeering activity or collection of unlawful debt, as those terms are defined in section 901(a) of the Organized Crime Control Act of 1970 (18 U.S.C. §§1961-1968);

"(B) a continuing criminal enterprise, as that term is defined in section 408 of the Controlled Substances Act (21 U.S.C. §848);

"(C) an offense under any of the following provisions of title 18, United States Code: section 201 (relating to bribery), section 224 (relating to bribery in sporting contests), sections 471-473 (relating to counterfeiting), section 659 (relating to theft from interstate shipment) if the offense is felonious, section 664 (relating to embezzlement from pension and welfare funds), sections 891-894 (relating to extortionate credit transactions), section 1084 (relating to the transmission of gambling information), section 1341 (relating to mail fraud), section 1343 (relating to wire fraud), sections 1461-1465 (relating to obscene matter), section 1503 (relating to obstruction of justice), section 1510 (relating to obstruction of criminal investigations), section 1511 (relating to obstruction of State or local law enforcement), section 1951 (relating to interference with commerce by threats or violence), section 1952 (relating to racketeering enterprises), section 1953 (relating to interstate transportation of wagering paraphernalia), section 1954 (relating to unfair welfare fund payments), section 1955 (relating to prohibition of illegal gambling businesses), sections 2314 and 2315 (relating to interstate transportation of stolen property), sections 2341-2346 (relating to trafficking in contraband cigarettes), or sections 2421-2424 (relating to white slave traffic);

"(D) an offense under title 29, United States Code, section 186 (relating to restrictions on payments and loans to labor organizations) or section 501(c) (relating to embezzlement from union funds); or

"(E) an offense involving the felonious manufacture, importation, receiving, concealment, buying, selling, or otherwise dealing in narcotic or other dangerous drugs, punishable under any law of the United States.

"(c) The provisions of this section shall be liberally construed to effectuate its remedial purpose.

"(d) Nothing in this section shall supersede any provision of Federal, State or other law imposing criminal penalties or affording civil remedies in addition to those provided for in this section.

"(e) Violations of this section shall be investigated by the Federal Bureau of Investigation, the Drug Enforcement Administration, and the Internal Revenue Service, as appropriate.

"(f) There is extraterritorial jurisdiction over the conduct prohibited by this section.".

(b) The table of sections at the beginning of chapter 95 of title 18 is amended by adding at the end the following new item: "1956. Laundering of monetary instruments".

PART B - FINANCIAL BRIBERY

Sec. 102. (a) Chapter 11 of title 18, United States Code, is amended by striking out section 215 and all that follows through section 216 and inserting in lieu thereof the following:

"§215. Bribery regarding financial operations

"(a) Whoever knowingly—
"(1) offers, gives, or agrees to give anything of value to any person with intent—
"(A) to influence any official action to be taken by; or
"(B) to induce the violation of a legal or fiduciary duty by;
such person as a director, officer, employee, agent, or attorney of a national credit institution; or
"(2) solicits, accepts, or agrees to accept anything of value from another—
"(A) because of any official action to be taken by, or any violation of a legal or fiduciary duty to be committed by, such person as a director, officer, employee, agent, or attorney of a national credit institution; or
"(B) that is given with the specific intent described in paragraph (1) of this subsection;
shall be punished as provided in subsection (b) of this section.

"(b) The punishment for an offense under this section is—

"(1) if the value of the thing offered, given, solicited, accepted, or agreed to be given or accepted, in violation of subsection (a) of this section, is greater than $250—

"(A) a fine of not more than $250,000 or imprisonment for not more than five years, or both, if the offender is an individual; or

"(B) a fine of not more than $1,000,000 if the offender is other than an individual; and

"(2) in any other case—

"(A) a fine of not more than $100,000 or imprisonment for not more than one year, or both, if the offender is an individual; and

"(B) a fine of not more than $250,000 if the offender is other than an individual.

"(c) As used in this section—

"(1) the term 'national credit institution' means—

"(A) a bank with deposits insured by the Federal Deposit Insurance Corporation;

"(B) an institution with accounts insured by the Federal Savings and Loan Insurance Corporation;

"(C) a credit union with accounts insured by the Administrator of the National Credit Union Administration;

"(D) a Federal home loan bank or a member, as defined in section 2 of the Federal Home Loan Bank Act (12 U.S.C. §1422), of the Federal home loan bank system;

"(E) a Federal land bank, Federal intermediate credit bank, bank for cooperatives, production credit association, and Federal land bank association;

"(F) a small business investment company, as defined in section 103 of the Small Business Investment Act of 1958 (15 U.S.C. §662); and

"(G) a bank holding company as defined in section 2 of the Bank Holding Company Act of 1956 (12 U.S.C. §1841) or a savings and loan holding company as defined in section 408 of the National Housing Act (12 U.S.C. §1730a);

"(2) the term 'official action' means a decision, opinion, recommendation, judgment, vote, or other conduct involving an exercise of discretion in the course of administration, employment, agency, or representation; and

"(3) the term 'anything of value' means any direct or indirect gain or advantage, or anything that might reasonably be regarded by the beneficiary as a direct or indirect gain or advantage, including a direct or indirect gain or advantage to another person, but such term does not include bona fide salary, wages, fees, or other compensation paid in the usual course of business.

"(d) There is extraterritorial jurisdiction over an offense under this section.

"§216. Graft in financial operations

"(a) Whoever knowingly—

"(1) offers, gives, or agrees to give anything of pecuniary value to any person with intent to reward such person for an official action taken by, or any legal or fiduciary duty violated by, such person as a director, officer, employee, agent, or attorney of a national credit institution; or

"(2) solicits, accepts, or agrees to accept anything of pecuniary value from another—

"(A) because of any official action taken by, or any legal or fiduciary duty violated by, such person as a director, officer, employee, agent, or attorney of a national credit institution; or

"(B) that is given with the specific intent described in paragraph (1) of this subsection;

shall be punished as provided in subsection (b) of this section.

"(b) The punishment for an offense under this section is—

"(1) if the value of the thing offered, given, solicited, accepted, or agreed to be given or accepted, in violation of subsection (a) of this section, is greater than $250—

"(A) a fine of not more than $250,000 or imprisonment for not more than three years, or both, if the offender is an individual; and

"(B) a fine of not more than $1,000,000 if the offender is other than an individual; and

"(2) in any other case—

"(A) a fine or not more than $100,000 or imprisonment for not more than six months, or both, if the offender is an individual; and

"(B) a fine of not more than $250,000 if the offender is other than an individual.

"(c) As used in this section—

"(1) the terms 'national credit institution' and 'official action' have, respectively, the meanings given those terms in section 215 of this title; and

"(2) the term 'anything of pecuniary value' means anything of value, as defined in section 215 of this title—

"(A) in the form of money, a negotiable instrument, a commercial interest, or anything else the primary significance of which is economic advantage; or

"(B) that has a value in excess of $100.

"(d) There is extraterritorial jurisdiction over an offense under this section.".

(b) The table of sections at the beginning of chapter 11 of title 18, United States Code, is amended by striking out the item relating to section 215 and all that follows through the item relating to section 216 and inserting in lieu thereof the following:

"215. Bribery regarding financial operations.
"216. Graft in financial operations.".

TITLE II—CURRENCY AND FOREIGN TRANS- ACTIONS REPORTING ACT AMENDMENTS

Sec. 201. Section 5318 of title 31, United States Code, is amended—
(1) by inserting "(a)" after "Sec. 5318.";
(2) by inserting ", except as provided in subsection (c)" before the semicolon at the end of paragraph (1);
(3) by striking out "and" at the end of paragraph (2);
(4) by redesignating paragraph (3) as paragraph (4);
(5) by inserting after paragraph (2) the following:
"(3)(A) examine any books, papers, records, or other data of domestic financial institutions pursuant to the recordkeeping and reporting requirements under this subchapter;
"(B) summon an officer or employee of a financial institution, or any person having possession, custody, or care of the reports or records required under the subchapter, to appear before the Secretary of the Treasury or his delegate at a time and place named in the summons and to produce such books, papers, records, or other data, and to give testimony, under oath, as may be relevant or material to such inquiry; and
"(C) take such testimony of the officer, employee, or person having possession of the relevant reports or records, under oath, as may be relevant or material to such inquiry; and"; and
(6) by adding at the end thereof the following:
"(b) The purposes for which the Secretary of the Treasury may take any action described in paragraph (3) of subsection (a) include the purpose of investigating any offense connected with the administration or enforcement of this subchapter, section 21 of the Federal Deposit Insurance Act, section 411 of the National Housing Act, or chapter 2 of Public Law 91-508.
"(c)(1) The Secretary of the Treasury may not delegate the powers conferred by subsection (a)(3) to an appropriate supervising agency.

"(2) A summons may be issued under subsection (a)(3)(B) only by, or with the approval of, the Secretary of the Treasury or a supervisory level delegate of the Secretary of the Treasury.".

Sec. 202. Section 5319 of title 31, United States Code, is amended by inserting before the period at the end of the first sentence the following: ", or when the Secretary has reason to believe that making such information available to the agency would further or facilitate the exercise of the Secretary's supervisory or regulatory functions under this subchapter".

Sec. 203. (a) Section 5321(a) of title 31, United States Code, is amended—

(1) by striking out the first sentence of paragraph (1) and inserting in lieu the following: "A domestic financial institution, and a partner, director, officer, or employee of a domestic financial institution, willfully violating this subchapter or a regulation prescribed under this subchapter (except section 5315 of this title or a regulation prescribed under section 5315) or causing such a violation is liable to the United States Government for a civil penalty of not more than—

"(A) the amount of the transaction where the violation involves a transaction reporting requirement, or

"(B) "$10,000 for any other violation."; and

(2) by adding at the end thereof the following:

"(4) A person willfully violating the provisions of section 5314 of this title or of a regulation prescribed under section 5314 is liable to the United States Government for a civil penalty of not more than the amount of the foreign transaction or foreign account involved in the violation.".

(b) Subsection (a) of section 5322 of title 31, United States Code, is amended by striking out "$1,000, or imprisoned for not more than one year, or both" and inserting in lieu thereof "$250,000, or imprisoned for not more than five years, or both".

(c) Subsection (b) of section 5322 of title 31, United States Code, is amended—

(1) by striking out "activity involving" and inserting in lieu thereof "activities that involve, but are not limited to,"; and

(2) by striking out "5" and inserting in lieu thereof "10".

(d) Subsection (a)(1) of section 5316 of title 31, United States Code, is amended—

(1) by inserting ", or attempts to transport or have transported," after "transports or has transported" in paragraph (1); and

(2) by striking out "more than $5,000" and inserting in lieu thereof "more than $10,000".

(e) Subsection (a) of section 5317 of title 31, United States Code, is amended—

(1) by inserting "(1)" after "(a)"; and

(2) by adding at the end the following new paragraph:

"(2) A customs officer may stop and search, without a search warrant, a vehicle, vessel, aircraft, or other conveyance, envelope or other container, or person entering or departing from the United States with respect to which or whom the officer has reasonable cause to believe there is a monetary instrument being transported in violation of section 5316 of this title.".

(f) Chapter 53 of title 31, United States Code, is amended by adding at the end thereof the following new section:

"§5323. Rewards for informants

"(a) The Secretary of the Treasury may pay a reward to a person who provides information which leads to the collection of a criminal fine, civil penalty, or forfeiture, which exceeds $10,000, for a violation of this subchapter.

"(b) The Secretary shall determine the amount of a reward under this section. The Secretary may not award more than 25 percent of the net amount of the fine, penalty, or forfeiture collected or $150,000, whichever is less.

"(c) An officer or employee of the United States, a State, or a local government who provides information described in subsection (a) in the performance of official duties is not eligible for a reward under this section.".

(g) The table of sections at the beginning of chapter 53 of title 31, United States Code, is amended by adding at the end the following new item:

"5323. Rewards for informants.".

Sec. 204. Section 5312(a)(5) of title 31, United States Code, is amended to read as follows:

"(5) 'United States' means the States of the United States, the District of Columbia, and, when the Secretary prescribes by regulation, the Commonwealth of Puerto Rico, the Virgin Islands, Guam, the Northern Marianas, American Samoa, the Trust Territory, any other territory or possession of the United States, or a military or diplomatic establishment.".

TITLE III—WIRETAP AMENDMENTS

Sec. 301. Section 2516 of title 18, United States Code, is amended—

(1) by inserting "section 1956 (laundering of monetary instruments)," after "section 1955 (prohibition of business enterprises of gambling)," in subsection (c);

(2) by striking out "or" at the end of subsection (f);

(3) by redesignating subsection (g) as subsection (h); and

(4) by inserting the following new subsection after subsection (f):

"(g) a violation of section 5322 of title 31, United States Code (dealing with the reporting of currency transactions); or".

TITLE IV—RIGHT TO FINANCIAL PRIVACY ACT AMENDMENTS

Sec. 401. (a) Subsection (c) of section 1103 of the Right to Financial Privacy Act of 1978 (12 U.S.C. §3403(c)) is amended to read as follows:

"Notification of existence, and disclosure, of relevant information in records; Federal preemption

"(c) Nothing in this chapter shall preclude any financial institution, or any officer, employee, or agent of a financial institution, from notifying a Government authority that such institution, or officer, employee, or agent has information which it believes may be relevant to a possible violation of any statute or regulation, and thereafter disclosing such information to that Government authority, regardless of whether a subpoena, summons, search warrant, or formal written request has been issued under the provisions of this chapter. The provisions of this subsection and any regulations promulgated thereunder shall preempt any provision of any constitution, law, or regulation of any State or political subdivision thereof, as well as any administrative or judicial interpretation of such provision, that is not identical to the provisions of this subsection and regulations thereunder, and that is more restrictive of disclosure to a Government authority concerning a possible violation of any statute or regulation than the provisions of this subsection and regulations promulgated thereunder.".

(b) Subsection (c) of section 1117 of the Right to Financial Privacy Act of 1978 (12 U.S.C. §3417(c)) is amended to read as follows:

"Good-faith defense

"(c) Any financial institution, or officer, employee, or agent thereof, making a disclosure of the financial records of a customer, or information contained in such records, pursuant to this chapter in good-faith reliance upon a certificate by any Government authority, or in good-faith belief that such records or information may be relevant to a possible violation of any statute or regulation, shall not be liable to the customer for such disclosure or for any failure to notify the customer of such disclosure.".

*   *   *

EXPLANATION

TITLE I

Section 101 would amend title 18 by adding a new substantive offense to the provisions of chapter 95 of title 18. Subsection (a) of the proposed section 1956 would make punishable the conduct of a transaction involving one or more monetary instruments in, through, or by a financial institution, if the person conducting the transaction intends, broadly speaking, to advance the interests of any person engaging in certain specified types of unlawful activity, or knows or has reason to know that the monetary instruments represent income or proceeds of various criminal offenses characteristic of organized criminal groups. The principal elements that would have to be established to prove a violation of the proposed section 1956 are set forth below:

1. Conducts. Money laundering frequently involves more than one deposit, withdrawal, exchange of funds, or other transaction in the effort to disguise or conceal the sources of those funds from the scrutiny of law enforcement agencies. For this reason, the term "conducts" is intended to encompass all acts—even those highly ministerial in nature—that introduce such funds into the financial system, direct them through the system, and ultimately withdraw them from the system either for investment in legitimate enterprises or reinvestment in illegal activities. In addition, the term "causes to be conducted" is intended to include not only those acts involving the supervision and direction of the

operations of money laundering schemes, but also the acts of criminals to enlist the aid of such persons to launder the income and proceeds of their illegal activities.

2. Transaction. This term is intended to include all means by which monetary instruments or electronically transferred funds may be moved throughout the financial system, whether the transaction is effected within or outside the physical confines of a financial institution. Such means would encompass face-to-face transactions; credit card or automatic teller machines owned or operated for the benefit of a financial institution; mail, common carriers, messengers, or bailees; telephone, telegraph, wire, radio, or television communications or any other form of electronic funds transfer; and any other method by which a customer may have debits or credits charged or assigned to an account on his behalf by a financial institution.

3. Monetary instruments. This term is intended to include all items that come within the definitions of the term "monetary instruments" that are set forth in the Currency and Foreign Transactions Reporting Act ("CFTRA") (31 U.S.C. §5312(a)(3)) and the Treasury Department regulations promulgated thereunder (31 C.F.R. §103.11).

4. Financial institution. This term is intended to encompass all agencies, branches, or offices within the United States doing business in one or more of the capacities listed in the definition of the term "financial institution" set forth in the CFTRA (31 U.S.C. §5312(a)(2)) and the Treasury Department regulations promulgated thereunder (31 C.F.R. §103.11). Because of the frequency with which they have been used to launder funds from drug trafficking and other illegal activities, casinos are intended to be included in this definition, as the Treasury Department has recently proposed for purposes of the reporting and recordkeeping requirements of the CFTRA. See 49 Fed. Reg. 32,861 (Aug. 17, 1984).

5. Engaging in or affecting commerce. This term is intended to extend the reach of section 1956 to the maximum extent consistent with Congress's power to regulate under the Commerce Clause.

6. Scienter. Section 1956 is not intended to proscribe mere inadvertent conduct by any person, whether an officer or employee of a financial institution or other person. It requires proof of either of two formulations of *scienter*: (1) that the person had the intent to promote, manage, establish, carry on, or facilitate the promotion, management, establishment, or carrying on, of an unlawful activity; or (2) that the person had knowledge or reason to know that the monetary instruments

represent income derived, directly or indirectly, from any unlawful activity, or the proceeds thereof.

The first formulation's use of the words "promote, manage, establish, carry on, or facilitate the promotion, management, establishment, or carrying on" is intended to permit the courts to draw on the body of judicial interpretations of identical language in subsection (a)(3) of the Travel Act (18 U.S.C. §1952(a)(3)). Its use of the term "unlawful activity," however, is intended solely to refer to the definition of that term in subsection (b) of this title, and not to the definition of an identical term in the Travel Act. As a general matter, this formulation is more likely to apply to the mental state of a person who oversees or supervises the activities of a group of persons who are collectively engaged in money laundering.

The second formulation is expressly intended to include the concepts of "conscious avoidance of knowledge," "deliberate ignorance," and "willful blindness" in the terms "knowledge or reason to know." *See generally, e.g., United States* v. *Jewell,* 532 F.2d 697 (9th Cir.), *cert. denied,* 426 U.S. 951 (1976). This formulation is intended to make clear that either a subjective or an objective standard of intent may be chosen for proof: that the person either knew in his own mind, or ought to have known (*i.e.,* that a reasonable man in that person's position would have known), that the monetary instruments were income or proceeds of unlawful activity. *See generally* W. LaFave & A. Scott, *Criminal Law* §127, at 193 (1972). This alternative set of standards is used with some frequency in title 18 offenses. *See, e.g.,* 18 U.S.C. §§2511 (concerning interception and disclosure of wire or oral communications), 2512 (concerning manufacture, distribution, possession, and advertising of wire or oral communication intercepting devices). As a general matter, this formulation is more likely to apply to lower-level participants who are more immediately and directly involved with effecting the transactions, even if they have had no personal contact with the criminals who procured the services of the money laundering group.

Under either of these formulations, the language should in no way be construed to require proof beyond a reasonable doubt of each element of an offense before that offense may be considered an "unlawful activity" within the meaning of this section.

Subsection (c) of the proposed section 1956 is intended to encourage courts to construe the provisions of this section as liberally as possible consistent with the rule of lenity.

Subsection (d) of the proposed section 1956 is intended to permit the independent application of any other provisions of Federal, state, or other law concerning criminal penalties or civil remedies. This provision would, for example, permit the forfeiture of monetary instruments to the extent that forfeiture has been, or may hereafter be, authorized under Federal law.

Subsection (e) is intended to make possible both joint and separate investigations by any and all of the Federal law enforcement agencies that are most likely to take an active interest in detecting and investigating money laundering schemes.

Subsection (f) is intended to make full use of Congress's power under the Constitution to proscribe certain conduct that occurs beyond the borders of the United States.

Section 102 would amend sections 215 and 216 of title 18 to proscribe various forms of bribery regarding financial operations and graft in financial operations. Because the provisions of this section are based upon those of H.R. 5872, which passed the House of Representatives on July 30, 1984, and Part F of Title XI of S. 1762, which passed the Senate on February 3, 1984, a detailed explanation of these provisions may be found in the legislative history of these bills.

TITLE II

Section 201 would amend section 5318 of the CFTRA to broaden the authority of the Secretary of the Treasury to obtain information for the purpose of ensuring compliance with the CFTRA and regulations thereunder. A new paragraph (3) of subsection (a) would authorize the Secretary to examine books, papers, records, or other data of domestic financial institutions, issue summonses to officers and employees of financial institutions and persons possessing records or reports required under the CFTRA, and to take testimony from those summoned. Subsection (b) would permit the Secretary to take any of the above actions for purposes that include investigating offenses connected with enforcement of the CFTRA, section 21 of the Federal Deposit Insurance Act, section 411 of the National Housing Act, or chapter 2 of the Bank Secrecy Act. Subsection (c) would limit the authority of the Secretary to delegate the powers conferred by subsection (a)(3). These provisions are based on the provisions of section 1 of S. 2579, introduced by Senator Alphonse D'Amato on April 12, 1984.

Section 202 would amend section 5319 of the CFTRA to permit the Secretary of the Treasury to make information in reports filed under section 5313, 5314, or 5316 of the CFTRA (currently, CTRs, CMIRs, and FBARs) to another Federal agency when the Secretary has reason to believe that making such information available to the agency would further or facilitate the exercise of the Secretary's supervisory or regulatory powers under the CFTRA. At present, under section 5319 and the regulations thereunder the Secretary may make such information available to another agency only if the head of the agency makes a written request that states "the particular information desired, the criminal, tax or regulatory investigation or proceeding in connection with which the information is sought and the official need therefor." 31 C.F.R. §103.43. Unlike the financial records of a financial institution or its customers, the reports required under sections 5313, 5314, and 5316 of the CFTRA are submitted to, and are the property of, the Treasury Department. Accordingly, the Treasury Department should have the discretion to provide information in its CFTRA reports to other Federal agencies when it has reason to believe that those agencies can assist it in fulfilling the Department's statutory responsibilities under the CFTRA (*e.g.*, by investigating criminal violations of the CFTRA).

Subsection (a) of section 203 would amend section 5321 of title 31 to increase the maximum civil penalty which can be imposed under the CFTRA from $1,000 in all cases to the amount of the transaction where the violation involves a transaction reporting requirement, and to $10,000 in all other cases. Subsection (a) would also permit the Secretary to impose, in the case of a person willfully violating the provisions of section 5314 of title 31 or a regulation thereunder, a civil penalty of not more than the amount of the foreign transaction or foreign account involved in the violation. This section is based upon section 2 of S. 2579.

Subsection (b) of section 203 would amend subsection (a) of section 5322 of title 31 by increasing the maximum criminal penalty from a $1,000 fine or one year's imprisonment to $250,000 and five years' imprisonment. Subsection (c) is based upon subsection (b) of section 901 of S. 1762 and subsection (b) of section 2 of H.R. 6031.

Subsection (c) of section 203 would amend subsection (b) of section 5322 of title 31 by increasing the maximum term of imprisonment, in caes where a person has violated the CFTRA or a regulation thereunder while violating another Federal law or as part of a pattern of illegal activity involving transactions of more than $100,000 in a twelve-month period, from five to ten years. Subsection (c) would also respond to the decision in *United States* v. *Dickinson*, 706 F.2d 88 (2d Cir. 1983), by adding language that makes clear that the "pattern of illegal activity" that serves as the predicate for the enhanced criminal penalties must include, but need not be limited to, transactions of more than $100,000 in a twelve-month period.

Subsection (d) of section 203 would amend subsection (a)(1) of section 5316 of title 31 by increasing the minimum amount of money being transported in or out of the United States that must be reported in a CMIR from more than $5,000 to more than $10,000. This change would bring the jurisdictional amounts in the CFTRA into conformity and reduce the burden of compliance for both the Treasury Department and international travelers.

Subsection (e) of section 203 would amend subsection (a) of section 5317 of title 31 to provide U.S. Customs officers with explicit authority to search, without a search warrant, persons, vehicles, vessels, aircraft, and other conveyances, envelopes, or other containers entering or departing the United States if the officer has reasonable cause to believe that a monetary instrument is being transported in violation of section 5316 of title 31. Subsection (f) of section 203 would add a new section 5323 to title 31 that would permit the Secretary of the Treasury to pay rewards for information leading to a criminal fine, civil penalty, or forfeiture if the fine, penalty, or forfeiture exceeds $10,000. No reward could exceed the lesser of $150,000 or 25 percent of the net amount of the fine, penalty, or forfeiture collected. Subsections (d)-(g) of section 203 are based on subsections (c)-(f) of section 901 of S. 1762 and subsections (c)-(f) of section 2 of H.R. 6031.

Section 204 would amend subsection (a)(5) of section 5312 of title 31 to clarify the scope of the definition of the term "United States." Section 204 is based upon section 3 of S. 2579.

TITLE III

Section 301 would amend section 2516 of title 18 to permit the proposed section 1956 of title 18 and section 5322 of title 31 to serve as predicate offenses for the issuance of judicial orders authorizing or approving interceptions of wire or oral communications in conformity with the provisions of Title III of the Omnibus Crime Control and Safe Streets Act of 1968.

TITLE IV

Subsection (a) of section 401 would amend subsection (c) of section 1103 of the Right to Financial Privacy Act ("RFPA") to permit financial institutions, as well as their officers, employees, or agents, to disclose to a Government authority only such information as they believe may be relevant to a possible violation of any statute or regulation. At present, section 1103 permits financial institutions to notify a Government authority only that they have information which may be relevant to a possible violation of a statute or regulation. Because a law enforcement agency can rarely, if ever, justify opening a formal investigation, and thereafter complying with the elaborate procedures required by the RFPA, on the basis of an unsupported assertion by a financial institution, section 1103 discourages both the agency from pursuing potential leads in money laundering cases and the financial institutions from contacting the agency. This state of affairs serves neither the interests of the legitimate financial community in discouraging the use of financial institutions by money launderers, nor the interests of law enforcement in ensuring compliance with the Bank Secrecy Act and other Federal statutes and regulations.

Subsection (a) also would add a provision that would preempt all state constitutions, statutes, regulations, or judicial decisions that appear to establish a more restrictive standard than the amended section 1103 of the RFPA for disclosures of information by financial institutions to a Government authority. Any state provision that established an equally or less restrictive standard would be unaffected by subsection (a).

Subsection (b) of section 401 would amend subsection (c) of section 1117 of the RFPA to permit a financial institution, or officer, employee, or agent thereof, against which a customer had brought a civil action under the RFPA because of its disclosure of records or information to a Government authority, or because of its failure to notify the customer of such disclosure, to assert as an absolute defense that it had made the disclosure in good-faith belief that the records or information may be relevant to a possible violation of a statute or regulation. This amendment is necessary to give full effect to the provisions of the proposed section 401(a), by ensuring that financial institutions which seek to assist law enforcement agencies in detecting and investigating criminal activities will not thereby inadvertently expose themselves to potentially substantial liability under the RFPA.

ENDNOTES

[1] A recent survey of data from United States Attorneys' offices, conducted by the Department of Justice's Executive Office for United States Attorneys at the request of the Commission, disclosed that during fiscal years 1981 to present, ten banks have been convicted of violations of the Bank Secrecy Act, as a result of either trials or guilty pleas. At present, there are forty-one active investigations of banks for assorted currency violations, in United States Attorneys' offices. Memorandum from C. Madison Brewer, Director, Office of Management Information Systems and Support, Executive Office for United States Attorneys, Department of Justice, to James D. Harmon, Jr., Executive Director, President's Commission on Organized Crime (Oct. 4, 1984).

In a survey conducted by the Organized Crime and Racketeering Section of the Department of Justice, two financial institutions and twelve officers or employees of financial institutions were indicted in Organized Crime Strike Force cases from January 1, 1980 to September 19, 1984. Both institutions and five of the individuals were subsequently convicted; one person pleaded guilty to a criminal information; three individuals were acquitted; one individual officer or employee had the case dismissed; and two individuals have cases pending. The available data indicate that both institutions and two of the individuals were charged with violations of the Bank Secrecy Act. Letter from Gerard T. McGuire, Deputy Chief, Organized Crime and Racketeering Section, Department of Justice, to Rodney G. Smith, Deputy Executive Director, President's Commission on Organized Crime (Sept. 20, 1984).

[2] For a detailed discussion of the offshore bank issue, see Crime and Secrecy: The Use of Offshore Banks and Companies: Hearings Before the Permanent Subcomm. on Investigations of the Senate Comm. on Governmental Affairs, 98th Cong., 1st Sess. (1983).

[3] Michele Sindona, an Italian tax and corporate attorney, established a financial holding company in 1960 through which he purchased a number of American businesses. During the 1960s and 1970s, Vatican financial ministers placed several billion dollars in cash and stock through Sindona-controlled investment institutions. In 1982, Banco Ambrosiano of Milan, the largest private banking group in Italy, collapsed due to a $1.4 billion exposure in loans to several mysterious Panamanian companies which had been endorsed by the Vatican Bank, Institute per le Opere di Religione. Sindona was involved with Banco Ambrosiano's

president and other members of a secret Italian Masonic lodge known as Propaganda Due, or P2, in sending Banco Ambrosiano money to support political causes in Latin America. Financial support for P2 activities allegedly came from the Mafia's narcotics trafficking as well, and was laundered through fiduciary accounts in Switzerland by Sindona. On September 24, 1984, Sindona was extradited to Italy to stand trial for the murder of Giorgio Ambrosoli, the liquidator of Sindona's financial empire. Sindona is now serving a twenty-five year sentence for causing the collapse of the Franklin National Bank in New York with the resulting loss of more than $40 million. In a deposition taken by the Commission on August 29, 1984, Sindona provided the Commission with extensive information concerning the use of offshore banks to conceal or disguise the source and application of funds.

[4] The term "money laundering" is derived from the argot of criminals, who refer to "dirty" or "black" cash being "washed" so that it can be used openly.

[5] 12 U.S.C. §§1829b, 1951-1959; 31 U.S.C. §§5311-5322. In Congressional testimony concerning the Bank Secrecy Act, Robert Morgenthau, formerly the United States Attorney in the Southern District of New York and now the District Attorney in New York County, warned that domestic banks were often made accomplices to organized crime:

> Abuse of secret foreign accounts is no longer limited to members of organized criminal syndicates and hoodlums. . . . Many American banks opened branches in the foreign tax havens so that their customers could also avail themselves of the advantages provided by secret bank accounts. These American banks sought out, exploited and asserted the protections of local secrecy laws as vigorously as the foreign banker . . . .

> As a result of this expanded activity by American banks, transfers of funds, illicit and otherwise, through domestic banks on the way to secret foreign bank accounts became commonplace; the domestic clearing and correspondent facilities of United States banks became essential in many instances to the carrying out of illegal schemes involving foreign banks.

Bills to Amend the Federal Deposit Insurance Act to Require Insured Banks to Maintain Certain Records, to Require that Certain Transactions in United States Currency be Reported to the Department of the Treasury, and for Other Purposes: Hearings on S. 3678 and H.R. 15073 Before the Subcomm. on Financial Institutions of the Senate Comm. on Banking and Currency, 91st Cong., 2d Sess. 244 (1970) (statement of Robert M. Morgenthau).

[6] As demonstrated in hearings conducted earlier this year by the Subcommittee on Crime of the House Committee on the Judiciary, casinos have been used with increasing frequency to launder substantial amounts of currency. Neither the Bank Secrecy Act nor the regulations explicitly define casinos as "financial institutions" that are subject to the requirements of the Act. To the extent that casinos carry out duties that are similar or related to those carried out by other types of financial institutions (*e.g.*, exchange of currency), the Act vests the Secretary of the Treasury with sufficient authority to subject casinos to its requirements. *See* 31 U.S.C. §5312(a)(2)(U). To date, the Treasury Department has not amended its regulations to include casinos, although it has recently issued a notice of proposed rulemaking on this issue. *See* 49 Fed. Reg. 32,861 (Aug. 17, 1984).

[7] 31 U.S.C. §5322(b). A 1983 decision by a panel of the United States Court of Appeals for the Second Circuit, however, has tended to limit the utility of this enhancement provision. In *United States* v. *Dickinson*, 706 F.2d 88, 91 (2d Cir. 1983), the panel construed the phrase "a patten of illegal activity involving transactions of more than $100,000" to mean that the enhancement provision could properly be applied only when the pattern of illegal activity involved "repeated violations of the [Act] itself, related to each other, and together involving more than $100,000." The panel's construction of the phrase thus limits the applicability of the enhancement provision to a pattern of illegal activity under the Act.

[8] 31 U.S.C. §5321(a)(1), (2).

[9] *See, e.g.*, General Accounting Office, "Better Use of Currency and Foreign Account Reports by Treasury and IRS Needed For Law Enforcement Purposes," April 6, 1979 (GGD-79-24); General Accounting Office, "Bank Secrecy Act Reporting Requirements Have Not Yet Met Expectations, Suggesting Need for Amendment," July 23, 1981 (GGD-81-80).

[10] National Narcotics Intelligence Consumers Committee, Narcotics Intelligence Estimate - 1983 [hereinafter cited as 1983 NNICC Estimate] at 51.

[11] Because this case is now on appeal, details and identifying data concerning the defendants have been withheld.

[12] The Use of Casinos to Launder the Proceeds of Drug Trafficking and Organized Crime: Hearings Before the Subcomm. on Crime of the House Comm. on the Judiciary [hereinafter cited as Casino Laundering Hearings], 98th Cong., 2d Sess. (1984) (testimony of W. Hunt Dumont, United States Attorney, District of New Jersey).

[13] Letter from Larry B. Sheafe, Acting Deputy Assistant Secretary (Enforcement), Department of the Treasury, to James D. Harmon, Jr.,

Executive Director, President's Commission on Organized Crime (Aug. 29, 1984) [hereinafter cited as Treasury Department Letter].

[14] The agencies participating in this analysis have explained the limitations on its usefulness:

> The data presented in these findings must be viewed with utmost caution. They are intended only to provide orders of magnitude and indicate direction of change. Numbers associated with the illegal drug trade—consumption, prices, imports, etc.—are subject to large errors. Information of even less reliability is available on the amount of drug-related money moving through international financial markets. Estimates of the current situation often are based on the subjective view of experts. New information or statistical analysis could alter these findings significantly. Nonetheless, the data presented here are adequate to portray the problem at hand and to support the findings. . . . The dollar values are provided only to place the problem in general perspective and should not be considered definitive.

[15] National Narcotics Intelligence Consumers Committee, Narcotics Intelligence Estimate 64 (1982).

[16] This individual is not further described because criminal charges against him are still pending.

[17] Casino Laundering Hearings (testimony of Gary D. Liming, Deputy Assistant Administrator for Intelligence, Drug Enforcement Administration).

[18] 1983 NNICC Estimate at 36.

[19] Id. at 37.

[20] See Hearings Before the House Select Comm. on Narcotics Abuse and Control, 98th Cong., 2d Sess. (1984) (testimony of Dominick L. DiCarlo, Assistant Secretary, Bureau of International Narcotics Matters, Department of State).

[21] Mangan, "The Southeast Asian Banking System," DEA Quarterly, Winter 1984, at 7.

[22] 31 U.S.C. §5313(a).

[23] See 31 U.S.C. §5319; 31 C.F.R. §103.43 (1984).

[24] See 31 C.F.R. §103.46(a) (1984).

[25] 31 C.F.R. §103.46(b) (1984).

[26] Exams admits that it steers clear of checking currency exchange houses such as Deak-Perera to avoid "legal problems." See United States v. Deak Perera & Co., 566 F. Supp. 1398 (D.D.C. 1983), in which the District Court denied enforcement of an IRS recordkeeping summons issued to Deak-Perera for production of documents reflecting transactions with a particular customer. An IRS Revenue Agent had performed a Bank Secrecy Act compliance examination at Deak-Perera's

Washington, D.C. office in May 1980, and compiled a list of 83 transactions involving $25,000 or more, noting the customer's name, address and other identifying information and referring the list to respective IRS field offices to facilitate audits of the customers' tax returns. An IRS Special Agent, who had information from an independent source with respect to other transactions in precious metals by a particular individual, caused a summons to issue to Deak-Perera for any and all records pertaining to the customer. In denying enforcement of the summons, the Court found that the Bank Secrecy Act and implementing regulations do not authorize a general sharing of incidental intelligence acquired in a compliance audit, even intra-agency as in the case of the IRS, if to do so would violate a subject's legitimate expectations of privacy. *Id.* at 1402. Thus, Exams' compliance audit staff is effectively precluded from referring potential Bank Secrecy Act and tax violations discovered during routine examinations to the logical investigative agency, IRS Criminal Investigation Division, further hampering Exams' regulatory function.

[27] *See, e.g.,* 12 U.S.C. §1784.

[28] In general, a bank may exempt from the reporting requirements deposits or withdrawals of currency by an established depositor, provided the depositor is a U.S. citizen, operates a retail-type business, and is paid in substantial portion by currency. Transactions which may be exempted must be in amounts commensurate with the customary conduct of the lawful, domestic business of that customer. *See* 31 C.F.R. §103.22(b), (c) (1984). Records of exemptions granted by an institution must be kept in a centralized list, and must include sufficient information to identify the exempted account holder. *See* 31 C.F.R. §103.22(e) (1984).

[29] *E.g.,* 12 U.S.C. §1818(c)(1).

[30] *E.g.,* 12 U.S.C. §1818(g)(1).

[31] *E.g.,* 15 U.S.C. §78o(b)(4).

[32] The NCUA discontinued periodic reporting to the Treasury Department in 1983 after letter notice to the Department, although compliance exams are still conducted at member institutions.

[33] *See* Fed. R. Crim. P. 6(e).

[34] *See generally* 26 U.S.C. §6103.

[35] Treasury Department Letter.

[36] 31 U.S.C. §5319 states, in pertinent part:

The Secretary of the Treasury shall make information in a report filed under section 5313 [concerning CTRs], 5314 [concerning foreign financial agencies], or 5316 [concerning CMIRs] of [title 31] available to any agency on request of the head of the agency. The report shall be available for a purpose consistent with those sections or a regulation prescribed under those sections.

The Treasury Department regulation implementing this provision states that the request must be "made in writing and stat[e] the particular information desired, the criminal, tax or regulatory investigation or proceeding in connection with which the information is sought and the official need therefor." 31 C.F.R. §103.43 (1984).

[37] *See* Hearings Before the Subcomm. on General Oversight and Renegotiation of the House Comm. on Banking, Finance and Urban Affairs, 98th Cong., 2d Sess. (1984) (testimony of John Walker, Assistant Secretary (Enforcement and Operations), Department of the Treasury).

[38] *Compare, e.g., United States* v. *Rojas,* 671 F.2d 159, 163 (5th Cir. 1982), *and United States* v. *Cutaia,* 511 F. Supp. 619, 624-25 (E.D.N.Y. 1981), *with United States* v. *Gomez-Londono,* 553 F.2d 805, 810 (2d Cir. 1977).

[39] In other instances, financial institutions have declined to provide Federal law enforcement authorities with information relevant to money laundering investigations on the ground that state law precludes them from revealing such information. According to a survey of state laws governing access to information on bank transactions, conducted by the Institute of Judicial Administration at the request of the Commission, only California, Nevada, Oregon, and Tennessee have adopted financial privacy statutes which include provisions explicitly permitting the voluntary disclosure of information when the financial institution suspects illegal activity, to state authorities. Institute of Judicial Administration, State Laws Governing Access to Information on Bank Transactions 7 (1984).

These provisions, however, fail to state whether financial institutions may also disclose customer records to agencies other than state or local entities. Moreover, state judicial decisions in California, Colorado, Illinois, and Pennsylvania have interpreted state constitutional provisions to infer a right of privacy in customer records, while in ten states, state judicial decisions have indicated that a financial institution has an implied contractual duty to its customers and depositors to keep their records confidential, in the absence of authorization by law or by the customer or depositor. *Id.* at 11.

[40] 12 U.S.C. §3403(c).

[41] 52 U.S.L.W. 4815, 4819 (U.S. June 18, 1984).

[42] Letter from Robert C. Bonner, United States Attorney, Central District of California, to James D. Harmon, Jr., Executive Director, President's Commission on Organized Crime (Sept. 21, 1984), enclosing Memorandum from Brian A. Sun, Assistant United States

Attorney, Central District of California, to Robert C. Bonner (Sept. 14, 1984).

[43] *Compare, e.g., United States* v. *First Bank,* 737 F.2d 269 (2d Cir. 1984) (holding that under Supremacy Clause, notice provisions of Connecticut Financial Privacy Act preempted by provisions of Internal Revenue Code governing IRS administrative summons), *with* In re The Grand Jury Subpoena East National Bank of Denver, 517 F. Supp. 1061 (D. Colo. 1981) (rejecting Supremacy Clause argument challenging judicially-created state expectation of privacy in bank records; asserting that failure of financial institution to give notice to customer will create risk of lawsuit in state court for such failure).

[44] One account places both Michele Sindona and Tommaso Buscetta at the meeting. Luigi DiFonzo, St. Peter's Banker 86 (1983).

[45] 416 U.S. 21, 46-47 (1974).

[46] Although S.1762 proposed to include the criminal provisions of the Bank Secrecy Act as a predicate for prosecution under the Racketeer Influenced and Corrupt Organizations (RICO) statute (18 U.S.C. §§1961-1968), this draft legislation would obviate the need for amendment of the RICO statute to permit its substantial financial penalties to be levied against money launderers.

www.ingramcontent.com/pod-product-compliance
Lightning Source LLC
Chambersburg PA
CBHW031949190326
41519CB00007B/734